THE SCHOOL OF LIFE is dedicated to exploring life's big questions: *How can we fulfil our potential? Can work be inspiring? Why does community matter? Can relationships last a lifetime?* We don't have all the answers, but we will direct you towards a variety of useful ideas – from philosophy to literature, psychology to the visual arts – that are guaranteed to stimulate, provoke, nourish and console.

THESCHOOLOFLIFE.COM

By the same author:

The Age of Absurdity
New and Selected Poems
Embracing the Ordinary

By Henri Bergson:

Essai sur les données immédiates de la conscience
Matière et mémoire
Le Rire
L'Évolution créatrice
L'Énergie spirituelle
Les Deux Sources de la morale et de la religion
La Pensée et le mouvant
Mélanges
Key Writings

By William James:

The Dilemma of Determinism
What is an Emotion?
The Principles of Psychology
Psychology: The Briefer Course
The Will to Believe
On a Certain Blindness in Human Beings
Talks to Teachers
The Varieties of Religious Experience
The Energies of Men
The Letters of William James

BERGSON

Great Thinkers on Modern Life

Michael Foley

PEGASUS BOOKS
NEW YORK LONDON

BERGSON

Pegasus Books LLC
80 Broad Street, 5th Floor
New York, NY 10004

First Pegasus Books edition 2015

ISBN: 978-1-60598-676-0

10 9 8 7 8 6 5 4 3 2 1

Printed in the United States of America
Distributed by W. W. Norton & Company, Inc.

CONTENTS

INTRODUCTION

....

In my youth, satirical humour seemed the most appropriate response to a venal world and this interest in the theory and practice of comedy led me to Henri Bergson's book *Laughter: an Essay on the Meaning of the Comic*. I was not entirely convinced by Bergson's theories but I liked his scathing comments on the stultifying effects of convention and social life, which he defined as 'an admiration of ourselves based on the admiration we think we are inspiring in others'.

I poked around in the Bergson oeuvre – but was disappointed. In his other work he displayed no satirical disgust or, despite the comedy book, wit, and his key work, *Creative Evolution*, proposed that the meaning of life was something called *élan vital*, which struck me as a vague, mystical concept. As a consequence of a scientific education, I respected only thinking that was hard-edged, logical and clear. For me, the intention of mysticism was to enshroud the world in mist.

So *au revoir*, *Henri*. I forgot about Bergson in the following decades of adult life, which was meant to comprise derisive laughter launched at the world from a rented garret but somehow turned out to be the conventional entanglements of mortgage, job, wife and child. Satire was no longer enough and I turned to thinkers like Erich Fromm, whose marvellous little book, *The Art of Loving*, helped me to make a go of marriage, whose *The Sane Society* taught me social and political awareness, and whose *To Have and to Be* taught me that religion might be of use to non-believers, and that Buddhism in particular might offer practical lessons.

Much later, I learned from the twentieth-century philosophy of mind that memory and the self are processes rather than fixed entities – and suddenly this connected with the theories of particle physics, which claim that at the heart of matter there are in fact no particles but only processes. Then that connection made a further connection with the central Buddhist concept of 'no soul, no substance'. And, in a thrilling Eureka moment, philosophy, science and religion came together in the revelation that *everything is process . . . and everything is connected to everything else.* Or, to be more precise, that the cosmos is a vast unity of interpenetrating and interdependent processes, a gigantic mega process made up of maxi processes themselves made up of mini processes composed of micro processes – all the way in to the weird heart of matter and all the way out to the weird far end of our madly-expanding universe. And interacting with all this is the equally weird mega process of human consciousness, made up in turn of its own whirl of interpenetrating processes.

The concept that *everything* is process seemed to me an original insight, at least in Western thought. But my euphoria was soon tempered by the discovery that this was the central premise of process philosophy, a long-established and flourishing sub-genre with its own academic centres, professors and journals. On the other hand it was reassuring to discover that so many others shared the process view. I found that these ideas go back to Buddha and Heraclitus, who claimed that everything is fire and flow, and then it turned out that the true founder of modern process philosophy was none other than the thinker I had rejected so long before – Henri Bergson. 'Substance is movement and change,' he announced unequivocally. 'There are changes, but underneath the changes no things which change: change does not require a support. There are movements, but no inert or invariable object which moves: movement does not imply a mobile.' The crucial thing, according to Bergson, was to accept this movement and become part of it: 'Philosophy can only be an effort to dissolve again into the Whole.'

In other words, it is all about process and unity. *Bonjour encore, Henri.* But who was this guy?

Henri Bergson (1859–1941) was the second child of Michael Bergson, a Polish composer/pianist who came to Paris to make his name but never succeeded, and Kate Levinson, a Yorkshire woman of Irish descent.

Both father and mother were devout Jews, but Henri abandoned religion at a young age, possibly a response to being left in a boarding school while his parents took the other children to England, never to return. This early isolation may account for his independence and reserve, profound distrust of social life and insistence on the need to create and protect a deep self.

If rejecting Judaism was a rebellious act, it was his only one. Bergson seems to have desired only the conventional bourgeois life of career and family. Success at both school and university was followed by teaching secondary-level philosophy in the provinces, then lecturing in Paris and, once he was established, marriage, a daughter and an intimate, happy, intensely private family life. (He never spoke publicly of his wife and daughter, and after his death his widow complied with his wish to have all personal papers destroyed.)

Bergson's life-changing revelation of process came in 1884 when he was engaged in that most pleasurable of processes – walking.

All of the philosophy that begins with Plato . . . is the development of the principle that there is more in the immutable than in the moving, and we pass from the stable to the unstable by mere diminution. Now it is the contrary which is true.

(*La Pensée et le mouvant*, 1934)

In other words, Plato's influential concept of ideal unchanging forms that exist somewhere beyond the imperfect world was a fantasy expressing the human hunger for immutability and perfection. There is only this imperfect world and everything in it is constantly changing.

Bergson's first two books promoting this idea were received with polite interest in French academic circles – but in 1902 he discovered that for popular success there is nothing more effective than promotion by an enthusiastic and energetic American. Out of the blue came a letter from William James who, despite being celebrated and seventeen years older, acclaimed Bergson's second book, *Matière et mémoire*, as a masterpiece:

> It is a work of exquisite genius. It makes a sort of Copernican revolution . . . and will probably . . . open a new era of philosophical discussion. It fills *my* mind with all sorts of new questions and hypotheses and brings the old into a most agreeable liquefaction. I thank you from the bottom of my heart.
>
> (*The Letters of William James*, 1920)

This letter must have been enthralling for Bergson, who had found in James's work the two qualities he admired most – generosity and enthusiasm. And for me it was enthralling to discover that one of my favourite thinkers, James, was also a Bergson fan. This was no mere intellectual rapport, for when the two met they immediately hit it off. Despite being an international celebrity, James was entirely without self-importance and recognized similar humility in Bergson. As he wrote to a friend: 'So modest and unpretending a man but such a genius intellectually. I have the strongest suspicion that the tendency which he has brought to a focus will end by prevailing.'

For the next two years they corresponded regularly and when James died in 1910 Bergson wrote: 'No one loved truth with a more ardent love and no one sought it with a greater passion.' And throughout the rest of his long life Bergson kept a portrait of James in his study.

The extent of their mutual influence is the subject of much debate, but they seem to have been thinking on similar lines for a long time before becoming aware of each other. Indeed their ideas were so similar that I like to regard the two as a single thinker – 'James Bergson' – the French half more original, more impersonal and more focused on the implications of the process view; the American half more engaging, more personal and with wider-ranging interests. But both halves were equally interested in chance and possibility; freedom and determinism; consciousness, memory and attention; religion and mysticism; and both investigated these only as means of experiencing life more vividly.

James insisted that philosophy was worthless if it did not provide 'cash value'.

James was certainly right about Bergson prevailing. With the appearance of *L'Évolution créatrice* in French in 1907 and in English as *Creative Evolution* in 1911, Bergson became the most famous thinker in the Western world. (James welcomed this book with more impersonal understatement: 'O my Bergson, you are a magician and your book is a marvel, a real wonder'). In Paris people gathered outside windows, and even scaled ladders to reach upper windows, to catch a few words of his lectures. In London he became a media celebrity, much to the amazement of the English philosopher T. E. Hulme: 'We have not been able to buy even a sporting evening paper without finding in it an account of a certain famous philosopher.' And in 1913 Bergson caused one of New York's first traffic jams, when Broadway was brought to a standstill by crowds desperate to attend a lecture called *Spiritualité et Liberté*, delivered *in French*.

Perhaps even more astounding was Bergson's secret political mission on behalf of the French government. In 1917 he was despatched to the USA to persuade Woodrow Wilson to join the war on the side of the Allies. It was known that Wilson wanted to set up a League of Nations to promote world peace, and the French strategy was to suggest to Wilson that this would be more feasible if he had a place at the negotiating table after the war. Bergson, who was also a fervent advocate of a League of Nations, played on Wilson's intellectual vanity, treating him as a philosopher-king whose combination of idealism and power made him the only man capable of saving civilization. It is not known if Bergson's fortnight in Washington was decisive – but shortly afterwards Wilson took the USA into the war. Bergson returned to Washington for this development and at the end of the war served as the interpreter between the French and American leaders in the negotiations leading to the Treaty of Versailles.

Official recognition followed, with Bergson collecting the full set of French honours and in 1928 the Nobel Prize for literature. But his belief in the necessity of accepting change was soon to be tested to the limit. Rejected as an outdated establishment figure by the ambitious new boys like Sartre and Merleau-Ponty, his reputation as a thinker began to fade. Then his health failed. The great celebrant of mobility was left half paralysed by a rheumatic disorder. On top of this, all his public work came to nothing. The great advocate of internationalism saw the collapse of the League of Nations, which he had helped to found and had worked for, at the expense of his own work. The great campaigner for world peace was obliged to endure another world war and the occupation of France by the Nazis.

The Vichy government offered him exemption from the anti-Semitic laws as an 'Honorary Aryan' but he refused and went or, rather, was helped (in dressing gown and slippers, according to one account) to a police station to queue up in bitter cold to register as a Jew. As a consequence he was stripped of all his honours, which at least permitted him to prove his claim that these had never been important and that what matters, even at the age of eighty-two, is the free act. Shortly afterwards he died of bronchitis, his last words those of a lifelong teacher and learner: 'Gentlemen, it is five o'clock. The class is over.'

The class was over for Bergson but it is still very much in session for the many who have absorbed and applied his ideas. Not only were these ideas central to the oldest religion (though Bergson seems to have been unaware of the similarity to Buddhist thought), they are also everywhere in the newest science (though the scientists appear to be unaware of Bergson). There have been Bergsonian developments recently in neuro-science, psychology, physics, chemistry and biology, for instance theories of consciousness, memory and personal identity, the psychology of cognition and emotion, the physics of elementary particles and fields, the chemistry of non-equilibrium reactions and the biology of living organisms.

And in the arts Bergson's ideas were enthusiastically embraced by the modernist movement and influenced, among others, T. S. Eliot, Marcel Proust, Paul Valéry, Gertrude Stein, Wallace Stevens, Robert Frost, George

Bernard Shaw, Virginia Woolf, Katherine Mansfield and Willa Cather.

But what relevance have these ideas for the world of marriage, mortgage and office desk? What can mere ideas offer to those who fear that their experience is pitifully limited, even non-existent? Bergson agreed that experience is crucial – this is his main theme – but argued that it is not so much a matter of what as of how – not a matter of embarking on travels, adventures and love affairs but of experiencing everyday reality more intensely. Experience may be deepened as well as widened – and concepts such as unity and process can be the key to such deepening. If we could experience reality as 'continuous and indivisible' and as 'mobility itself', Bergson insisted, then our everyday lives would be 'illuminated and nourished'.

1

LEARNING TO SWING ALONG
WITH THE PROCESS

....

One of the most common characteristics of depression is a sense of monotony and stale repetition, a crushing sameness that seems as though it can never change and never provide sustenance. On many occasions I have had this terrifying thought: 'Nothing is happening; I am gaining no experience; I will die without ever having really lived.' The revelation that everything is process dispels this illusion of monotony. As Bergson put it, 'the same does not remain the same'.

In the process view nothing is fixed, nothing is final, and no circumstances ever repeat in the same way. Even God, in traditional theology the ultimate unmoved mover, becomes for Christian process thinkers the ultimate movement. Not even God may stay the same.

Such a vision can be vertiginous, as Bergson conceded:

Before the spectacle of this universal mobility some may be seized by dizziness. They are accustomed to terra firma, cannot get used to the rolling and pitching and must have fixed points of attachment for thought and existence. They believe that if everything passes nothing exists; and that if reality is mobility, it has already ceased to exist at the moment of perception – it eludes thought. The material world, they say, will disintegrate, and the mind will drown in the torrential flow.

(*La Pensée et le mouvant*, 1934)

But, as in all white-knuckle rides, the dizziness is also exhilarating:

Reality no longer appears essentially static, but affirms itself dynamically, as continuity and variation. What was immobile and frozen in our perception is warmed and set in motion. Everything comes to life around us, everything is revitalized within us. A great impulse sweeps forward beings and things. We feel ourselves uplifted, borne along, carried away. We are more fully alive and this increase of life brings with it the conviction that grave philosophical enigmas can be resolved and even perhaps that they may not be raised, since they arise from a frozen vision of the real and are only the translation, in terms of thought, of a certain artificial weakening of our vitality.

(*La Pensée et le mouvant*, 1934)

So change is the essence of process. But our contemporary attitudes to change are an unhealthy mixture of worship and denial. The worship is for novelty, change for the sake of change, and the denial is of the inevitable organic changes in matter, both inanimate and living, and especially of ageing and death. Bergson argued eloquently for acceptance of the inevitable:

> I believe that if one were convinced of the reality of change and made an effort to grasp it, everything would be simplified . . . Not only would philosophy gain, but our everyday life – I mean the impression things make upon us and the reaction of our intelligence, sensibility and will – would perhaps be transformed and, as it were, transfigured. The point is that usually we look at change but do not see it. We speak of change, but do not think about it. We say that everything changes, that change is the very law of things: yes, we say it and repeat it; but these are only words, and we reason and philosophize as though change did not exist. In order to think change and see it, it is necessary to brush away a veil of many prejudices, some of them artificial, created by philosophical speculation, and others natural to common sense.
>
> (*La Pensée et le mouvant*, 1934)

One of these common-sense prejudices is attachment to *things,* to what Bergson called 'the logic of solids':

> The human intellect feels at home among inanimate objects, and especially among solids, where our action discovers its fulcrum and our work its tools; our concepts have been formed on the model of solids and our logic is pre-eminently the logic of solids.
>
> (*L'Évolution créatrice*, 1907)

Things are reassuringly visible, stable and durable. We love things and surround ourselves with them. And we ourselves yearn to be people of substance, in every sense. We believe, fundamentally and passionately, in *stuff*. But in fact there is no stuff. One of Bergson's most daring assertions was to deny the solidity of matter:

> We have no reason for representing the atom to ourselves as a solid . . . We may still speak of atoms; the atom may still even retain its individuality for the mind which contemplates it; but its solidity and inertia dissolve either into movements or lines of force whose reciprocal solidarity brings back universal continuity.
>
> (*Matière et mémoire*, 1896)

This sounds like the view of a twenty-first-century physicist but was written long before the splitting of the atom, never mind quantum mechanics and particle and field physics, which tell us that there is nothing substantial at the heart of things, only some sort of weird dance of energy.

Most Western thought before Bergson accepted the primacy of substance but, although Bergson does not seem to have been aware of this, and certainly does not acknowledge it in his writing, Eastern thought always put process before substance. One of the central Buddhist concepts is *samsara*, meaning 'incessant motion'. Everything in the universe is fluid, dynamic, constantly changing.

But we yearn to be people of substance and believe not just in substantial *things* but in a substantial *self*, a soul, a constant, fundamental essence that endures throughout life, and even, for many, throughout all eternity. It is a nasty shock to be told that this is also an illusion. Bergson:

> Our psychic life ... imagines a formless ego, indif-ferent and unchangeable, on which it threads the psychic states which it has set up as independent entities. Instead of a flux of fleeting shades merging into each other, it perceives distinct and, so to speak, *solid* colours, set side by side like the beads of a necklace; it must then suppose something solid, a thread, to hold the beads together.
>
> (*L'Évolution créatrice*, 1907)

The William James version of this is that 'thought is itself the thinker', a concept that could be extended to define the experiencer as what is experienced and the knower as what is known. It was James who first came up with the term 'stream of consciousness' to describe mental activity – but even this suggests a process too linear and orderly. 'Vortex of consciousness' would be better – because, as in a vortex of water above a drain, the content is constantly and turbulently changing but the shape remains relatively stable. In consciousness this apparently stable form is the self and the stability makes it seem permanent – until it suddenly goes down the plughole with a gurgle of outrage and despair.

This loss of the essence of soul may be as alarming as the loss of the solidity of matter – but it can also be liberating and consoling. One of Buddhism's central insights is that acceptance of 'no self' (*anattā*) helps to temper the demands and obstinacies of the ego. So many everyday problems come from feelings of superiority, self-importance and self-righteousness, or from refusals to adapt. 'I'm too good for this,' we say. Or: 'I'm just the way I am.' To both these claims the process view responds with a resounding 'No, you're not.' Bergson and James remained largely unaffected by international fame because it is harder to become self-important if aware that there is really no self to begin with. So if we too could abandon this belief in a precious, unique essence we might feel less superiority and more solidarity.

In fact we could transform all our relationships by understanding them not as static links but as dynamic processes. We tend to regard the connections implied by spouse, parent, sibling and boss as unchanging and the associated emotions as end states. Constant flux is frightening, and as persistent as the yearning for solidity is the yearning for finality, for absolute end states – love, nirvana, knowledge, wisdom or definitive English grammar.

One of the most common illusory end states is the present. Our current beliefs, conventions and taboos always seem to be the inevitable and final culmination of history. So history becomes like a Hollywood quest movie, a slow, stumbling, wrongheaded and wayward, but always fated and unstoppable, progress to the Holy Grail and happy ending of the present:

> Any judgement that is true now seems to us to have been always true. It does not matter that it had never been formulated: it existed by right before existing in fact. So we give every truth a retroactive effect. As though a judgement could have existed before the circumstances which made it possible!
>
> The consequences of this illusion are innumerable. Our estimate of people and events is wholly impregnated with a belief in the retrospective value of true judgement ... By the mere fact of having happened reality casts a shadow behind into the indefinitely distant past: it seems to have existed as a possible before its own realization. This error

falsifies our conception of the past and justifies our claim to anticipate the future.

(*La Pensée et le mouvant*, 1934)

The consequence is that we adopt a smug 'presentism' and love to scold history for being so incorrect. But the process view frees up the past, as well as the present, and future.

There are no unchanging objects or end states but when it comes to love, possibly the most complex of all relations, we often run into difficulties by believing in both of these – that romantic success is merely a matter of finding the right person, the object (as if!), and that this will automatically lead to the desired end state, love (an even more derisive, as *if*!).

And so it is again not surprising that both Bergson and James were happily married, for the process view dispels the illusion of 'happy marriage' as a final state of sitting hand in hand, gazing serenely at the sunset. Marriage is process and process is frequently turbulent. Bergson's private life remains a mystery but we know that the Jameses' marriage was not all fond handholding. Once, when the family were touring Europe and running short of money, William returned to their rented accommodation with two expensive oil paintings. His wife protested strenuously and there was an angry row, which ended with William going for a pair of scissors and cutting both paintings to pieces. Such is the nature of happy marriage.

We make similar misjudgements in that other fascinatingly complex relationship: power. Here the illusory object is the position of power and the illusory end state is the submission of the powerless. But, much to the consternation of dictators, generals and middle managers, power is entirely dynamic, draining away from those who use it unwisely, and accruing to those who do merit respect. This process is gradual and invisible – until suddenly the pillars of power collapse and the mighty edifice comes crashing down. So hardly anyone foresaw the fall of a series of communist dictators in 1989 or Arab dictators in 2011.

As Bergson pointed out, aversion to change makes it easy to miss the imperceptible but crucial changes going on all the time:

> It is expedient to disregard this uninterrupted change, and to notice it only when it becomes sufficient to impress a new attitude on the body, a new direction on the attention. Then, and then only, we find that our state has changed. The truth is that we change without ceasing, and that our state itself is nothing but change.
>
> (*L'Évolution créatrice*, 1907)

So alertness to process in general can bring many benefits – and it is even more satisfying to swing along with an actual process, as William James advised:

Wherever a process of life communicates an eagerness to him who lives it, there the life becomes
genuinely significant. Sometimes the eagerness is
more knit up with the motor activities, sometimes
with the perceptions, sometimes with the imagination, sometimes with reflective thought. But
wherever it is found, there is the zest, the tingle, the
excitement, of reality; and there *is* 'importance' in
the only real and positive sense in which importance
ever anywhere can be.

(*On a Certain Blindness in Human Beings*, 1899)

The most satisfying processes are often the simplest –
walking, swimming, reading, writing, thinking. Bergson,
despite his austere appearance, regarded dancing as the
most satisfying physical process. If he were a celebrity
today, instead of a century ago, he would surely be invited
to participate in *Strictly Come Dancing* and might become
a surprise hit:

Let us consider the feeling of grace. At first it is only
the perception of a certain ease, a facility in outward
movement. And as those movements which prepare
the way for others are easy, we are led to find a
superior ease in the movements we can foresee, in
the present attitudes which indicate and, as it were,
prefigure future attitudes. If jerky movements are
lacking in grace, it is because each is self-sufficient

and does not announce those which follow. If curves are more graceful than broken lines, the reason is that, while a curved line changes its direction at every moment, every new direction is indicated in the preceding one. Thus the perception of ease in motion becomes the pleasure of the flow of time, of holding the future in the present. A third element comes in when the graceful movements submit to a rhythm and are accompanied by music. For the rhythm and measure, by allowing us to foresee to a still greater extent the movements of the dancer, make us believe that we now control these. As we guess almost the exact attitude which the dancer will take, she seems to obey us when she actually takes it: the regularity of the rhythm establishes a kind of communication, and the periodic returns of the measure are like so many invisible threads by which we move this imaginary puppet. Indeed, if the movement stops for an instant, our hand in its impatience cannot refrain from reacting, as though to replace the rhythm which has taken complete possession of our thought and will. Thus a kind of physical sympathy enters into the feeling of grace.

(*Essai sur les données immédiates de la conscience*, 1889)

2

LEARNING TO TUNE IN TO
THE MELODY OF DURATION

....

The natural processes that we have come to fear are driven by time and so time has become the enemy. There is never enough time, it passes too quickly and its passage destroys beauty, strength and intelligence. Then, most outrageous of all, time gets disgusted by the wreck it has produced and dumps it in the recycling bin.

Bergson observed that we allay the terror of time and try to make it reassuring by applying the logic of solids and objectifying time as space, a comforting conversion of fluid to rigid and moving to stationary (it is significant that no one ever views space as time):

Throughout the history of philosophy time and space have been treated as similar; the procedure has been to study space, to determine its nature and function, and then apply the conclusions to time. So theories of space and time became counterparts and to pass from one to the other it was necessary to change only one word and replace 'juxtaposition' by

'succession' . . . So when we invoke time it is space
which answers the call.

(La Pensée et le mouvant, 1934)*

This may sound like irrelevant philosophical abstraction but Bergson's insight on time remains timely because, in our own time, the conversion of time to space is remarkably common. When the psychologist Claudia Hammond conducted a survey of attitudes to time she discovered that many people do indeed spatialize, although not, as might be expected, by seeing time as a line, but by seeing it as a circle, a loop, an oval, even a spiral, or as a map, a clockface, a horseshoe, a river, or a row of dominoes with Saturday and Sunday represented by larger sizes. And Hammond *recommends* this sort of approach, though without clearly explaining the benefits.

The interesting question is whether this tendency is becoming more common – i.e. is it innate or culturally conditioned? It seems more likely to be conditioned because the human sense of time has gone from complete unawareness to total obsession. 'Time' is now the most-used noun in English, whereas many primitive peoples, for instance the Amondawa tribe of the Amazon and the Australian Aborigines, do not even have a word for it.

Bergson distinguished two versions of time – the measured, which he defined as clock time, and the experienced, which he defined as duration. Clock time, spatialized and uniformly calibrated, is obviously necessary, but only duration is authentic. The problem is that clock time increasingly dominates contemporary living, and duration is becoming harder to experience. 'What is duration within us?' Bergson asked. 'A qualitative multiplicity, with no relation to number; an organic evolution that may not be quantified.'

This warning is also timely. The last few years have seen the birth and dramatic growth of an evangelical movement known as the Quantified Self, which promotes, as the key to well-being, a self constantly measured and monitored in as many ways as possible. This movement, which began in the USA in 2007, now has organizations in fifty cities worldwide, including London, and spreads its message via meetings, films, literature and a website. The overt message is that quantification provides control over one's life, and the covert message is that this control will nullify time and enable the Quantified Self to live for ever. (Sometimes the covert message becomes overt, as with the card-carrying Quantified Selfer, Ian Clements, who hopes to write a book called *How to Live to 150*).

More generally, the dominance of quantified time is revealed by our contemporary obsession with time management. If Bergson had lived to 150 he would have told us that time management is indeed crucial but we have got it the wrong way round – we should learn not to manage time but to let time manage us. The advice to recover duration was an exhortation to consent to process and immerse in time. The paradox is that the only escape from time is in submission to time. When we are flowing along with a process, awareness of time disappears. And if, instead of fighting against time, we could go along gladly, then the flow might develop into something more graceful. Bergson loved music (no doubt a legacy from his musician father) and his favourite example of unity in process was a melody:

Real duration is what we have always known as time, but time perceived as indivisible. I do not deny that time implies succession. But I cannot admit that succession is presented to consciousness with the distinction of a 'before' and 'after' set side by side. When we listen to a melody we have the purest impression of succession we could possibly have – an impression removed as far as possible from that of simultaneity – and yet it is the very continuity of the melody and the impossibility of breaking it up which makes that impression upon us. If we divide it up into distinct notes, into so many 'befores' and 'afters', we are bringing in spatial images and infusing the succession with simultaneity: in space, and only in space, is there a clear-cut distinction between external parts. Moreover, I am aware that we normally place ourselves in spatialized time. We have no interest in listening to the uninterrupted humming of life's depths. And yet, that is where real duration abides.

(*La Pensée et le mouvant*, 1934)

Bergson offered no practical advice on how to experience real duration – but attendance to the humming of the depths sounds remarkably like the Buddhist practice of *Ānāpāna-sati*, respiration-mindfulness. William James made this connection:

Hatha Yoga processes, the postures, breathings . . . are manners . . . of breaking through the barriers which life's routine had concreted round the deeper strata of the will, and gradually bringing its unused energies into action.

(*The Letters of William James*, 1920)

So one way of recovering duration is to meditate. The traditional Buddhist method requires sitting cross-legged on the floor at dawn – but I see no reason to follow this (and James warned against attributing 'any sacramental value' to a particular exercise). We should all create our own rituals. I much prefer to sit on a sofa at dusk. The gradual fading of the light is a perfect example of process, 'succession without distinction', impossible to catch in action but impossible to miss in effect. And the effect, especially if accompanied by a glass of wine, can be mysterious, enchanted, a spell that encourages reconciliation with process and time. Then it is possible to hear a murmur counselling reversal of that famous rage of Dylan Thomas – no, no, do not rage . . . and yes, yes . . . *do* go gentle into that good night.

3

LEARNING TO HEED THE
WHISPERS OF INTUITION

....

If my major life decisions are based on rational analysis, as I believe they should be and are, why do I often
struggle to remember the reasons for these crucial
choices? How could I have forgotten the motives for
decisions with such far-reaching consequences? And
if my fundamental beliefs are based on a similarly
rational analysis, how can these have changed radically
over a lifetime?

Bergson's answer is that I have not forgotten the
reasons for decisions because these decisions were
never reasoned out in the first place. And my changing
beliefs have always seemed objectively rational because
they have been given ingenious rationalizations after
each change. Far from being the process of making
decisions and forming convictions, rational analysis is
more often retrospective justification. So such analysis,
and indeed all intellectual endeavour, is suspect.

'The intellect is unable to comprehend life,' Bergson
declared boldly, setting the fashion for anti-intellectual
intellectuals. 'Intellectual truth is a human invention

whose purpose is to use reality rather than to dwell in it.' And again this distrust of categories, concepts, theories and even of language itself is also central to Buddhist and indeed all Eastern thought. 'A name is merely the guest of reality,' Chuang-Tzu warned back in the fourth century BCE.

In particular, analysis in terms of linear logic encourages a deterministic view of life. Bergson conceded that such logic is appropriate in science: 'For the physicist, the same cause always produces the same effect.' But it is different for mental states:

> To say that the same inner causes will reproduce the same effects is to assume that the same cause can appear a second time in consciousness. Now, if duration is what we claim, deep-seated psychic states are radically heterogeneous and no two could be quite alike, since they are two different moments in a life history.
>
> (*Essai sur les données immédiates de la conscience*, 1889)

In other words, as Heraclitus told us long ago, no one steps into the same river twice.

In fact, since the discoveries of quantum mechanics, even physics has had to accept that the behaviour of elementary matter is acausal and becomes predictable only at the level of statistical aggregates. And the mind, with its massively parallel working, complex feed-back loops and deep embedding in the physical and emotional life of the body, makes a nonsense of linear logic and determinism. All through his work Bergson insisted on unpredictability and freedom:

> The discussions on free will would come to an end if we saw where we actually are, in a real duration where the idea of necessary determination loses all significance, since in duration the past continuously creates – along with the present, if only by being added to it – something absolutely new.
>
> (*La Pensée et le mouvant*, 1934)

Bergson did accept that predictability is a comforting illusion:

> The entire intellect rises in revolt against this idea of absolute originality and unforeseeability. For the essential function of intellect, as fashioned by evolution, is to guide conduct, to prepare for action, to foresee, for a given situation, the events which may follow from it, favourable or unfavourable. And so the intellect, applying its principle that 'like produces like', instinctively selects from the situation whatever matches something already known. This is how common sense envisages the future.
>
> (*L'Évolution créatrice*, 1907)

And the corollary of predictability as comfort is randomness as threat. William James identified, as a major obstacle to accepting unforeseeable process, fear of 'chance, the very name of which we are urged to shrink from as from a metaphysical pestilence'. We not only need to foresee what happens but to believe it has meaning and so we cannot bear to acknowledge that much is merely random. We would almost rather accept gross injustice than randomness. At least with injustice there is someone to blame. And good fortune is just as rarely recognized. For bad luck we blame others, and for good luck take the credit ourselves. But chance, according to James, should not just be grudgingly accepted but welcomed as a form of grace:

> Let us not fear to shout it from the house-tops if need be; for we now know that the idea of chance is, at bottom, exactly the same thing as the idea of gift ... its presence is the vital air which lets the world live, the salt which keeps it sweet.
>
> (*The Dilemma of Determinism*, 1884)

However, Bergson did acknowledge that much human behaviour is indeed predictable because it is the unthinking and automatic response of habit and conditioning, a reflex action of the utilitarian or social self. But every now and then we reject habit, conditioning, the temptation of practicality and the pressure of convention, to make decisions that are all the more compelling for seeming to defy reason:

> It is at the great and solemn crisis, crucial for our reputation with others, and even more with ourselves, that we choose in defiance of what is conventionally called a motive, and this absence of any obvious reason is the more striking the deeper our freedom goes.
>
> *(Essai sur les données immédiates de la conscience*, 1889)

So my life-changing decisions were never reasoned out but were the actions of the intuitive self, which frequently issues powerful vetoes without explanation. Bergson again:

> It seems to me that intuition often behaves in speculative questions like the demon of Socrates in practical life; at least it is felt most clearly in this way: it forbids. Faced with currently-accepted ideas, beliefs which seem self-evident . . . it whispers in the ear the word: *Impossible*!
>
> *(La Pensée et le mouvant*, 1934)

We should learn to trust these negative whispers – but intuition can also be positive:

> We define intuition as the *sympathy* which transports
> us into the interior of things in order to coincide with
> what is unique and inexpressible. Analysis, on the
> contrary, reduces things to what is already known.
>
> *(La Pensée et le mouvant*, 1934)

This form of sympathy is empathy, a word which did not exist when Bergson was writing but appeared shortly after, first in German (*Einfühlung*) and then in English. So positive intuition is the ability to identify with others and the world. As duration is the personal experience of process, so intuition is the personal experience of unity:

> Intuition may help us grasp what intelligence fails to
> provide . . . On the one hand it will use intelligence
> itself to show how intellectual frameworks cease
> to be strictly relevant; and on the other, by its own
> work, it will suggest a vague sense of what must
> take the place of such frameworks. So intuition may
> bring the intellect to recognize that life does not
> quite fit into categories; that neither mechanical
> causality nor finality can give a sufficient inter-
> pretation of *élan vital*. Then, by an expansion of
> consciousness and the sympathetic communication
> established with the rest of the living, it intro-
> duces us to life's reciprocal interpenetration and
> endlessly continuous creation. But though intuition

The lesson is that intuition lies somewhere in the
middle of a continuum with instinct at one extreme
and rational response at the other; it is instinct trained
by intelligence – or intelligence guided by instinct.
Both extreme reactions are suspect. The impulse may
be merely an animal desire and the reasoned response
a cunning justification. So how are we to make good
decisions? As in the old joke about how the elephant
puts its trunk in the crocodile's mouth – very carefully.
In the modern world we are probably more inclined to
trust the rational response but it is a mistake to believe
in a stable self that engages in rational analysis to make
rational decisions based on rational beliefs. Bergson
and James were almost a century ahead of psychology
in their realization that even our most fundamental
convictions are not entirely rational. Bergson:

The beliefs we hold most strongly are those we
would find it most difficult to justify, and our justi-
fications are seldom the reasons for adopting these
beliefs. In a sense we have adopted them without any
reason, for what makes them valuable is that they

match ... all our other ideas, and that ... we have
seen in them something of ourselves.

(*Essai sur les données immédiates
de la conscience*, 1889)

There are no entirely rational beliefs or decisions
– and of course no stable self in the first place.
Nevertheless, 'self', if understood entirely as process,
a series of psychological experiences, is a useful term
for the mental states, the thoughts and emotions and
behaviours, both reflex and willed, of the full human
organism. Bergson constantly distinguished between
two selves, meaning two levels of process – a superficial self whose reactions are socially conditioned and
a deep, intuitive self capable of empathy and free will.
This deep self is always in danger of being misrepre-
sented by the categorizing self, dismissed as irrelevant
by the utilitarian self and snuffed out as a threat to
popularity by the social self. How to protect and nurture
the crucial intuitive self?

We can perceive this self whenever, by a strenuous effort of reflection, we ... withdraw into
ourselves. Though we generally live and act outside
of ourselves, in space rather than in duration, and in
this way endorse the law of causality, which binds
the same effects to the same causes, we can nevertheless always get back into pure duration, whose

moments are internal and heterogeneous, and
where a cause can never repeat its effect because it
can never repeat itself.

(Essai sur les données immédiates
de la conscience, 1889)

And what is this 'strenuous reflection', this tuning in
to 'the continuous melody of our inner life', but, once
again, the practice of meditation? Again the answer is
your personal equivalent of spending time on the sofa
at dusk.

4

LEARNING TO LAUGH THROUGH DEPARTMENT MEETINGS

....

What happens when we fail to live in duration, no longer hear the inner melody and lose touch with the intuitive self? We become frozen, petrified – automatons, slaves of habit or convention or both. For the introvert, habit is the main danger and for the extrovert the tyrant is convention. So staying in and going out are equally dangerous.

Even the most liberating behaviour may quickly petrify into habit:

> Our freedom, in the very movements that affirm it, creates the developing habits that will stifle if it fails to be renewed by constant effort: it is dogged by automatism. The most living thought is petrified by expression. The word turns against the idea and the letter kills the spirit. Our most ardent enthusiasm, as it is externalized in action, is so naturally congealed into the cold calculation of interest or vanity, the one so easily assuming the shape of the

other, that we might well confuse them, doubt our sincerity, and even deny goodness and love, if we did not know that for a time the dead retain the features of the living.

(*L'Évolution créatrice*, 1907)

William James also warned against the stultifying effects of habit:

Could the young but realize how soon they will become mere walking bundles of habits, they would give more heed to their conduct while in the plastic state.

(*Psychology: The Briefer Course*, 1892)

On another occasion James gave a specific age for petrifaction onset:

Old fogyism begins at a younger age than we think. I am almost afraid to say so, but I believe that in the majority of human beings it begins at about twenty-five.

(*Talks to Teachers*, 1899)

Bergson, even more pessimistic, moved the onset back into childhood:

It seems possible that, after a certain age, we become impervious to all novel or fresh forms of joy, and the sweetest pleasures of the middle-aged are perhaps no more than a revival of the sensations of childhood, balmy zephyrs wafted ever more faintly by an ever-receding past.

(*Le Rire*, 1900)

There is certainly no doubt that the threat increases dramatically with age. I see the symptoms everywhere in my contemporaries and one of my most fervent wishes is to avoid a similar fate. I am petrified of becoming petrified. It is not just that this condition reduces the personal ability to experience and to enjoy but that it makes life so difficult and unpleasant for others: partners, family, colleagues and friends. The petrified are not easy to deal with. They have resolved to stop changing and so rage at the manifestations of change all around. And stinginess, both material and emotional, is likely to accompany this rage. The refusal to let anything in is accompanied by a refusal to give anything out.

I am in the high-risk category because of gender as well as age. Men seem especially prone to spiritual Alzheimer's. Nothing is changing, rages the angry young man; everything is changing, rages the angry old man, who retreats from the world and hardens into a shell of habit, eccentricity and peevishness. Generalizations about gender are dangerous but perhaps women are less at risk because they are more willing to immerse in life, to go with the flow and develop along with their children and then with their grandchildren. But this immersion makes women more vulnerable to the demands of social life, more likely to accept and uphold conventional ideas and behaviour. So men are at risk from habit and women from convention. We are all in danger all the time, as Bergson warned.

PETRIFACTION ALERT! You there, with the rictus of outrage, loosen up!

How to remain flexible, open and generous? Bergson argued that the comic sense has developed precisely to meet this need, that the social function of comedy is to correct petrifaction by making it laughable. The petri-fied person, unaware of automatism and eccentricity, becomes a figure of fun:

> Laughter must be something like this, a kind of *social gesture*. By the fear it inspires it restrains eccen-tricity, keeps awake and in mutual communication many second-order activities that might withdraw and go to sleep, and softens anything mechanical and inelastic in the social self. So laughter does not belong to aesthetics alone since it pursues uncon-sciously . . . a utilitarian purpose.
>
> (*Le Rire*, 1900)

According to Bergson, all comedy is based on the expo-sure of petrifaction – which seems to me to go too far. This comedy theory is a good example of Bergson's other theory on the inadequacy of theories. Comedy, one of the greatest human inventions, eludes not only Bergson's theory but all others as well. Every attempt to define comedy is a joke. And to see comedy as solely utilitarian is to make another mistake identified by Bergson himself – diminishing a vital impulse by forcing it into a category. Defining comedy as a form of social work misses its anarchic, subversive zest.

Nevertheless, Bergson had many insightful things to say on the subject. For instance, he pointed out that comedy, although it can be bitter and nihilistic, is a great restorer of oneness with the world:

> It is the function of comedy to repress any separatist tendency, to convert rigidity into plasticity, to readapt the individual to the whole.
>
> (*Le Rire*, 1900)

Yet, paradoxically, this comic oneness is attainable only by means of detachment:

> Characters in real life would never make us laugh if we could not follow their vagaries as we look down at a play from a seat in a box.
>
> (*Le Rire*, 1900)

Withdrawing from blind involvement in order to observe and study enables a different re-engagement enriched with understanding and empathy.

And Bergson reminded us that comedy is process. We tend to believe that some things are funny and others not, and that this distinction is final. But what a culture finds funny changes over time – as does the individual comic sense. When I saw the film *Billy Liar* back in the sixties I laughed till my chest hurt with the violence of the paroxysms – but when I saw it again recently I could barely raise a faint smile. Fortunately the opposite also happens. When I first read Proust I completely missed the droll humour and now I find him hilarious. Such change is inevitable but may also be positively directed. It is possible to develop a more sophisticated sense of comedy, in the way that the palate may be trained to appreciate better wine, with the thrilling difference that in comedy the sophisticated is no more expensive than the crude.

For Bergson, comedy becomes more sophisticated the closer it approaches real life:

> It is only comedy's lower forms, in light entertain-
> ment and farce, that are in striking contrast to reality:
> the higher it climbs, the more it approximates to
> life; in fact, there are scenes in real life so close to
> high-class comedy that the stage might adopt them
> without changing a single word.
>
> (*Le Rire*, 1900)

The coarse-grained variety invites us to guffaw at stereotypical characters in farcical situations; the more sophisticated product makes us wince at the spectacle of all-too-recognizable characters in all-too-recognizable environments. We laugh and groan at people just like ourselves exposing their woeful lack of self-knowledge. But this kind of comedy is much more difficult to create and therefore much less common, indeed rare, because it demands constant fanatical attention to detail. Everything has to look and sound exactly right to ring true:

> Comedy delights in specific terms, technical details, definite facts . . . And this is no accident but its very essence. A comedian is a moralist disguised as a scientist.
>
> (*Le Rire*, 1900)

5

LEARNING TO KNOW WHAT WE KNOW BUT DO NOT SEE THAT WE KNOW AND TO SEE WHAT WE SEE BUT DO NOT KNOW THAT WE SEE

....

Petrifaction not only makes us appear laughable to others but deprives us of vital experience of life. And while we may be able to avoid becoming a laughing stock, few are capable of avoiding perceptual blindness. 'Life requires us to wear blinkers,' Bergson said, and as a consequence of the utilitarian demands of everyday living, we see only what is immediately relevant and consider only what is immediately practical:

> What I see and hear of the outer world is purely and simply a selection made by my senses to guide my conduct; so what I know of myself is what comes to the surface, what participates in actions. My senses and my consciousness, therefore, give me only a practical simplification of reality.
>
> (*Le Rire*, 1900)

So our awareness of ourselves and our environment is woefully deficient. In particular there is a tendency to see what things have in common rather than what makes them unique, the source of a dispiriting sense of sameness. Similarly, there is a tendency to see people only as types:

> The *individuality* of things and people escapes us, unless it is to our material advantage to perceive it. Even when we do take note – as when we distinguish one person from another – it is not the individuality itself that the eye registers . . . but only one or two features that will make practical recognition easier. In short, we do not see the actual things themselves but in most cases confine ourselves to reading the attached labels.
>
> (*Le Rire*, 1900)

This experience of unrelieved sameness leads at first to a sense of futility and then to fatigue. William James:

> We live subject to inhibition by degrees of fatigue which we have come only from habit to obey . . . Compared with what we ought to be, we are only half awake.
>
> (*The Energies of Men*, 1907)

The feeling of futility arises from the conviction that dreary sameness is a fundamental feature of the world. Bergson:

How can eyes be asked to see more than they see? Our attention may enhance precision, clarify and intensify; but it cannot bring out what was not there in the first place. That is the objection – in my opinion refuted by experience. In fact, for hundreds of years there have been people whose function was precisely to see and make us see what we do not naturally perceive. These are the artists.

(*La Pensée et le mouvant*, 1934)

As process philosophy helps to dispel the sense of sameness through time, so the arts help to dispel the sense of sameness through type. Our categorizing tendency likes to put people in pigeon holes (often contemptuously, as 'the careerist', 'the philistine', 'the slob', 'the shrew' etc.), then notices only behaviour that fits with the simplistic classification and finishes by dismissing people as superficial, limited, predictable and boring. The equivalent in relationships is to see only the irritating aspects of the partner and then to turn this into a final, dismissive definition. It is common even to *want* others to behave badly in predictable ways in order to confirm our own good judgement and enjoy superiority and righteousness. Conversely, because we hate change and want people to stay in their labelled boxes, unexpected developments can be irritating. When I began writing thinky books a few years ago, the attitude of many old friends was: 'Who does he think he is, writing *philosophy*?'

A crucial function of the arts is to prevent, or break down, dismissive labelling and reveal the singular instead of the similar, the peculiar instead of the familiar, and the inscrutable instead of the understood. I have often been guilty of impatient dismissiveness but recently, under the influences of literature, process thinking and the gentle remonstrations of my wife, I have come to find even people I have known for a lifetime increasingly strange. And, strangely enough, the fact that they elude me has brought them closer; my inability to understand them makes them more understandable.

Bergson especially valued music and dance as the most visceral ways of immersing in duration. And after these he prized poetry for capturing rhythm in language. This privileging of rhythm excited me enormously because, as a practising poet, I have always believed that, contrary to the usual view of poetry as images, poetry is rhythm. Bergson acknowledged the importance of images but subordinated them to rhythm:

> The poet develops feelings into images and the images into words which translate the words by means of rhythm. In seeing these images we in turn experience the feeling which was their emotional equivalent: but we would never feel these images so strongly without the movement of the rhythm.
>
> (*Essai sur les données immédiates de la conscience*, 1889)

So poetry is rhythm, a form of armchair dancing for the solitary and stiff-limbed – and what better way to avoid petrifaction than to swing with the rhythm? Once again it is no surprise that both Bergson and James were poetry lovers.

And the poets appreciated Bergson right back. Three of the greatest poets of the great modernist period, Robert Frost, T. S. Eliot and Wallace Stevens, were influenced by his ideas (though Eliot later rejected Bergsonism). What excited them was Bergson's hunger for more direct and vital experience and his interpretation of imagination and intuition as empathy. And what excited *me* was discovering the extent of the influence on Wallace Stevens, one of my favourite poets – another electrifying connection. Bergson is all through Stevens like the message in a stick of rock. (Stevens regarded Bergson as the most important thinker since Plato, quoted him directly in several essays and used his ideas throughout his poetry and prose, for instance by defining life as 'motion' and nature as 'incessant creation'.)

One of the factors that made the modern age so great was just this ability to mix different disciplines. Both poetry and philosophy were strengthened by their mutual engagement – and both have been enfeebled by their subsequent retreat into niches. Later twentieth-century poetry took too literally the Bergson and James distrust of intellectualism and rejected *all* ideas as dangerous contamination. Revealing my own interest in philosophy has caused many poets to regard me with horror, pity and fear. But contemporary poetry could do with more intellectual vigour. And the general lesson is that every specialism could do with being revitalized by every other. For the individual the lesson is to transcend disciplines and genres. We ought to make use of every way of understanding the world.

As for fiction, Bergson is also all through Proust. And, writing in the 1890s, he actually predicted modernism by pleading for novels that would 'draw aside for a moment the veil which we interpose between our consciousness and ourselves' and reveal the richness and strangeness of our inner lives:

> Now if some bold novelist, tearing aside the cleverly woven curtain of our conventional ego, could reveal, beneath this appearance of logic, a fundamental absurdity, beneath this juxtaposition of simple states an infinite merging of a thousand different impressions which have already ceased to exist as soon as named, we would praise him for having known us better than we knew ourselves. This is not the case, however . . .
>
> (*Essai sur les données immédiates de la conscience*, 1889)

But it was soon to be the case. Step forward, James Joyce.

All Bergson's work is inspired by a desire to revitalize awareness of the two great unfathomable, interlocking immensities – human consciousness and the material universe it briefly inhabits. So he wanted fiction to reveal how we think but do not know that we think, and painting to reveal what we see but do not know that we see. His taste in painting was conservative – for once he was not ahead of the game – but his comments on the nature painting of Corot and Turner apply equally well to Van Gogh's chair, Cézanne's jug and Edward Hopper's motorway underpass:

> If we reflect deeply on what we feel as we look at a Turner or a Corot, we will find that we accept and admire them because we have already perceived something of what they show. But we perceived it without seeing. For us it was a brilliant and passing vision, lost in the host of those visions which, in our ordinary experience, become clouded by reciprocal interference and make up our habitual pale and colourless view of things. But the painter has isolated it, fixed it on canvas so well that from now on we will not be able to help seeing in reality what he saw.
>
> (*La Pensée et le mouvant*, 1934)

6

LEARNING TO ENHANCE PERCEPTION, MEMORY AND ATTENTION

....

The usual answer to the problem of limited experience is new places or new people – cruising in the Caribbean or in singles bars – but it is possible to experience more without relocation or divorce. This low-cost solution is the enlarging and enriching of perception. Bergson's lesson was that consciousness is an indivisible unity, with all its functions interdependent, and in particular that perception is crucially bound up with memory. The categorizing and partitioning tendency sees perception as a camera and memory as a film archive in a basement, with no dynamic connection between the two. Bergson, almost a century ahead of neuroscience, rejected the common notion of memory as passive storage:

> Memory is not a faculty of entering recollections in a register or putting them away in a drawer. There is no register, no drawer.
>
> (*Matière et mémoire*, 1896)

His intriguing theory was that all memory is like the muscle memory that enables the body to recall how to ride a bicycle or to swim. These muscle memories are not stored as representations and, similarly, the mind does not store recollections but in perceiving a situation instantly brings into play the appropriate previous mental responses, just like the body discovering itself on a bike or in the sea. So memory does not wait patiently in some dusty archive but is constantly and urgently pressing forward into perception, to the extent that the characteristic movement of memory is not from present into past but from past into present. In fact memory and perception are a dynamic duo, linked in continuous, hectic interplay:

> Our distinct perception is really like a closed circle in which the perception-image, going in towards the mind, and the memory-response, launched out into space, career along one behind the other.
>
> We must emphasize this point. Attentive perception is often represented as a series of processes which make their way in single file; the object exciting sensations, the sensations inspiring ideas and each idea setting in motion, one behind the other, associations more and more remote. So there is assumed to be a linear progress, with the mind departing further and further from the object. We maintain that, on the contrary, reflective perception is a *circuit*, in which all

the elements, including the perceived object itself, hold each other in a state of mutual tension as in an electrical circuit, so that no disturbance starting from the object can stop on its way and remain in the depths of the mind: it must always find its way back to the object from which it came.

(*Matière et mémoire*, 1896)

Here Bergson hit upon the concept of the feedback loop, one of those blindingly simple insights that suddenly illuminate so much. Many complex systems, for instance weather and the stock market, have defied explanation because they are driven by feedback loops rather than linear chains of cause and effect and require new forms of analysis.

So memory is much more than a portable address book and reference library. It is the basis of the intuition that whispers compellingly *yes* or *no*:

Memory, in practice inseparable from perception, imports the past into the present and contracts many moments into a single intuition.

(*Matière et mémoire*, 1896)

Indeed, far from being an occasionally-accessed archive, or even an enricher of perception and intuition, memory is a crucial part of *all* mental activity – and some contemporary psychologists now believe that the effectiveness of working memory is a better measure of mental ability than IQ.

William James, who pondered the mysteries of memory as deeply as Bergson, came to the conclusion that association is the key:

> The 'secret of a good memory' is thus the secret of forming diverse and multiple associations with every fact we care to retain. But this forming of associations with a fact, – what is it but thinking *about* the fact as much as possible? Briefly, then, of two men with the same outward experiences, *the one who thinks over his experiences most*, and weaves them into the most systematic relations with each other, will be the one with the best memory.
>
> (*Talks to Teachers*, 1899)

So intense thinking is crucial for a good memory – and a good memory is crucial for intense thinking. As with most worthwhile achievements, there are no shortcuts. James, practical as always, tried a range of memory-training techniques – and found them all a waste of time:

> The popular idea that 'the Memory', in the sense of a general elementary faculty, can be improved by training, is a great mistake.
>
> (*Talks to Teachers*, 1899)

The problem is that such training is artificial, requires no original thought and creates no authentic associations. However, James noticed an interesting phenomenon:

> Suppose we try to recall a forgotten name. The state of our consciousness is peculiar. There is a gap therein; but no mere gap. It is a gap that is intensely active. A sort of wraith of the name is in it, beckoning us in a given direction, making us at moments tingle with the sense of our closeness, and then letting us sink back without the longed-for term. If wrong names are proposed to us, this singularly definite gap acts immediately so as to negate them. They do not fit into its mould. And the gap of one word does not feel like the gap of another, all empty of content as both might seem necessarily to be when described as gaps. When I vainly try to recall the name of Spalding, my consciousness is far removed from what it is when I vainly try to recall the name of Bowles.
>
> (*The Principles of Psychology*, 1890)

I have this experience often and in my case the active gap or mould gives me an initial letter and sometimes also a number of syllables. The important point is that, even when a word or name cannot be recalled, *it is possible to know whether or not it is available to memory,* and so whether or not it is worth pursuing recall. In these cases I never look up the name but try to bring it back by thinking of as many associations as possible – and frequently the missing name does indeed pop up, though it can be hours or days later.

The memory work Bergson kept returning to was learning a new language. This has the advantage of revealing the limitations of language in general. Words that seem indispensable in the mother tongue turn out to have no equivalent, while the new language has wonderful words that ought to be in the mother tongue but are not. So, to escape from the cage of language, learn another language. However, the main advantage is the effect on attention and memory. Recent research suggests that Bergson was right to encourage language learning because bilingualism improves mental focus (i.e. paying attention) and reduces the risk of Alzheimer's (i.e. memory deterioration). The reasons are not clear but the multiple associations constantly created by a new language are surely a factor. I certainly intend to continue my largely-unsuccessful attempts to learn French and may even have Bergson to thank for not going gaga just yet.

For James, rich association was the distinguishing feature of a fine mind:

> The minds of geniuses are full of copious and original
> associations. The subject of thought, once started,

develops all sorts of fascinating consequences. The attention is led along one of these to another in the most interesting manner, and the attention never once tends to stray away.

In a commonplace mind, on the other hand, a subject develops much less numerous associates: it dies out then quickly; and, if the man is to keep up thinking of it at all, he must bring his attention back to it by a violent wrench.

(*Talks to Teachers*, 1899)

In other words the genius is merely someone who understands, profoundly and intensely, that everything is connected to everything else, and that the less familiar the connection, the more rewarding it is likely to be. For the non-genius majority, who constantly forget this basic truth in their utilitarian focus, the good news is that the products of genius may be used to improve association – yet another cash value of the arts. So looking at a great painting, for instance, triggers unexpected new connections and then creates a new memory, which later shoulders its way into perception, shouting, as you absent-mindedly look out the window: 'This is a Hopper you're seeing, goddammit – Hopper would have painted these rusty drainpipes and roof.' The exciting consequence is that the world becomes a free art gallery exhibiting, all year round, Hoppers, Picassos and Van Goghs.

Come to think of it, in this age of democracy why not become an artist oneself? Bergson, in a fit of evangelical exuberance, claimed that philosophy could turn us all into geniuses:

> What nature does from time to time for certain privileged individuals, could not philosophy, in another sense and another way, attempt for everyone? Under such circumstances the role of philosophy would be to lead us to a more complete perception of reality by a displacement of attention. It would mean turning attention *away* from the part of the universe that interests us for practical reasons and *towards* the parts that serve no practical purpose. This conversion of the attention would be philosophy itself.
>
> (*La Pensée et le mouvant*, 1934)

'Attention' is the key word in this passage. Attention is focused perception, perception at work. It is always difficult to attend to the here and now because firstly there *is* no here and now, only continual movement, and secondly, we have an innate orientation towards the future. Bergson:

> Nature has invented a mechanism for canalizing our attention in the direction of the future.
>
> (*La Pensée et le mouvant*, 1934)

Why did Nature go to such trouble? The mechanism may be due to consciousness emerging as a successful adaptation because of its ability to plan ahead.

But Bergson understood that attention is as much about attitude as about effort of will.

> It seems to come from within, and to indicate a certain attitude adopted by the intellect. But this is where the difficulty begins, for the idea of an intellectual attitude is not clear.
>
> (*Matière et mémoire*, 1896)

Attention, needless to say, is another complex, dynamic process connected to all other mental functions. There is no single form of attention and no single attention centre in the brain. But it may not be necessary to understand, only to appreciate its importance and to exercise it, in both senses of training and using. Since perception/attention and memory are linked in a feedback loop, improving attention will improve memory just as improving memory will improve attention. It would be interesting to test the hypothesis that poor memory is associated with low general awareness.

And this cultivation of an attentive attitude is the Buddhist precept of mindfulness or *sati* (which in the *Pali* language of Buddhism means, significantly, both attention and memory). The awakened one is always on the alert, though you would never guess this from

Buddhist iconography, where the Buddha, with his big belly, somnolent expression and half-shut eyes, looks as though he has just eaten a double portion of mutton biryani.

In Western thought William James has given the strongest assertion of the crucial role of attention. According to James, our experience of life is nothing other than what we have chosen to pay attention to, and the choice is decisive because experience is character:

> Our acts of voluntary attention, brief and fitful as they are, are nevertheless momentous and critical, determining us, as they do, to higher or lower destinies.
>
> *(Talks to Teachers*, 1899)

In a letter to James, Bergson wholeheartedly agreed:

> The more I think about the question, the more I am convinced that life is from one end to the other a phenomenon of attention.
>
> *(Key Writings*, 2002)

But it was James who suggested that, unlike memory, attention may be trained:

> The prescription is that *the subject must be made to show new aspects of itself; to prompt new questions; in*

a word, to change. From an unchanging subject the attention inevitably wanders away. You can test this by the simplest possible case of sensorial attention. Try to attend steadfastly to a dot on paper or on the wall. You presently find that one or the other of two things has happened: either your field of vision has become blurred, so that you now see nothing distinct at all, or else you have involuntarily ceased to look at the dot in question, and are looking at something else. But, if you ask yourself successive questions about the dot – how big it is, how far, of what shape, what shade of color etc.; in other words, if you turn it over, if you think of it in various ways, and along with various kinds of associates – you can keep your mind on it for a comparatively long time.

(*Talks to Teachers*, 1899)

This is putting into practice Bergson's theory of memory and perception strengthening and enriching each other in a feedback loop. But why focus on a *dot*? Why not on a great painting? For James the insignificance of the object was crucial because learning to attend to the insignificant is the essence of creativity:

This is what the genius does, in whose hands a given topic coruscates and grows.

(*Talks to Teachers*, 1899)

7

LEARNING TO BE, AND
BELONG TO, AN ORGANISM

....

If we wish to understand the meaning of life then a good place to start would surely be with life itself, the biological phenomenon. A human being is an organism, albeit a highly complex one, and therefore subject to an organism's possibilities and limitations. William James studied physiology before turning to philosophy and believed that any speculation on human beings should begin by understanding them as basically reactive organisms:

> The concrete facts in which a biologist's responsibilities lie form a fixed basis from which to aspire as much as he pleases to the mastery of universal questions.
>
> (Diary entry quoted in *William James* by Robert D. Richardson, 2006)

Bergson agreed:

Everything is obscure if we confine ourselves to mere manifestations, whether they are described as social or features of individual intelligence. But all becomes clear if we start by a quest beyond these manifestations for Life itself. Let us then give to the word biology the very wide meaning it should have, and perhaps will have one day.

(Les Deux Sources de la morale et de la religion, 1932)

Before reading Bergson and James I had an instinctive dislike of biology, a rationalist repugnance which Bergson explained as the human intellect's preference for the static over the moving: 'The intellect, so skilful in dealing with the inert, is awkward the moment it touches the living.' The intellect prefers to understand life by rendering it lifeless – by killing the frog to dissect it.

There is also the intellectual problem that, in a complex organism, the whole is never merely the sum of the parts and the parts are never entirely independent of the whole.

Thus it is that the complexity of functioning of the higher organisms goes on to infinity. The study of one of these organisms therefore takes us round in a circle, as if everything was a means to everything else.

(L'Évolution créatrice, 1907)

The intellect, accustomed to linear reasoning, finds this kind of merry circular dance a nightmare.

But for those of a rational and/or fastidious temperament, inclined to the odourless abstract and remote, the way back to smelly life is to remember that every living thing, the sensitive thinker included, is an organism. For me this organismic view of life has been as illuminating as the process view – and is indeed only a special case of this view. An organism is a hectic, almost frenetic, process, operating far from equilibrium in a ceaseless metabolism that seeks out and draws in nutrients, converts them to energy, expels waste, and uses the energy to reproduce, and to regulate and renew its parts, so that its make-up is constantly changing though its structure is relatively stable. When it has reproduced, the organism wears out and dies – and the organismic view reinforces the process view of transience. If the purpose of philosophy is to teach us to die, as has often been claimed, then a philosophy of the organism must be the best teacher. One of Bergson's most striking passages is this biblical vision of living beings arising from the dust and returning to it, though not before creating and nurturing the next generation:

Like eddies of dust raised by the wind in its passing, the living turn upon themselves, borne up by the great blast of life. Therefore they are relatively stable, and fake immutability so well that we treat each as a *thing* rather than a *process*, forgetting that the very permanence of their form is only the outline of a movement. At times, however, in a fleeting vision, the invisible breath that sustains them materializes before our eyes. We have this sudden illumination before certain forms of maternal love, so striking, and in most animals so touching, observable even in the solicitude of the plant for its seed. This love, in which some have seen the great mystery of life, may possibly give us the secret of life. It shows us each generation leaning over the next and allows us to see that the living being is above all a thoroughfare, and that the essence of life is in the movement by which life is transmitted.

(*L'Évolution créatrice*, 1907)

Dust thou art and unto dust shalt thou return – but in between it will be all go. Throughout its life the organism learns constantly from the environment, adapting its behaviour to optimize its situation – and every now and then the adaptations produce a structural change. And the higher organisms are networks of organs, themselves networks of cells, themselves networks of microscopic components – while the organism's network is closely coupled to its environmental network. One organism's waste is another's meat and two veg.

So there are no independent, isolated, finished organisms. The human version, comprised of cells, is itself a cell in the organism of society:

> The members of a civic community are connected together like the cells of an organism. Habit, supported by intelligence and imagination, introduces among them a discipline resembling, in the interdependence it establishes between separate individuals, the unity of an organism of cells.
>
> (*Les Deux Sources de la morale et de la religion*, 1932)

As Bergson repeated many times, 'each of us belongs as much to society as to himself'. What society obliges us to do will always change – but never the fact of this obligation:

> It is society that prepares for the individual the programme of the daily routine. It is impossible to live a family life, work in a profession, attend to the thousand and one cares of the day, do the shopping, go for a stroll, or even stay at home, without submitting to obligations. At every moment we have to choose, and we naturally decide on what accords with the rules. We are hardly conscious of this; there is no effort. Society has marked out a road; before us

it lies open and we follow; it would take more initia-
tive to cut across country.

*(Les Deux Sources de la morale
et de la religion*, 1932)

Nevertheless Bergson was always careful to avoid any
suggestion of biological determinism. Intelligence may
always overrule instinct:

An intelligent being bears within itself the means to
transcend its own nature.

(L'Évolution créatrice, 1907)

The social demands are inescapable but the individual
may become aware of these and occasionally depart
from the road. And, far from being determined, Life,
driven by a force Bergson defined as *élan vital*, ceaselessly invents and *creates*.

The more we study the nature of time, the more we
shall comprehend that duration means invention,
the creation of forms, the continual elaboration of
the absolutely new.

(L'Évolution créatrice, 1907)

This idea, that Life is its own creator and that creativity
is not a late aesthetic refinement but the very principle
of existence, was Bergson's most radical and inspiring

insight. Rejoice in the revelation that Life is not a dreary conformist but an exuberant Picasso.

> What is admirable *in itself*, what really deserves to inspire wonder, is the ever-renewed creation which reality, whole and undivided, accomplishes in its advance.
>
> (*L'Évolution créatrice*, 1907)

For a long time science dismissed this notion as mystical claptrap. But recently it has validated Bergson's insight with a theory of emergence, or self-organization, which explains how life may develop from inanimate matter, complexity from simplicity and order from chaos. For living systems, powered by chemical reactions far from equilibrium, the constant adaptations to the environment may at certain critical points produce something entirely new and unpredictable. Here is the molecular biologist, Stuart A. Kauffman, sounding exactly like Bergson: 'In the new scientific worldview I'm describing, we live in an emergent universe of ceaseless creativity in which life, agency, meaning, consciousness and ethics . . . have emerged. Our entire historical development as a species . . . has been self-consistent, co-constructing, evolving, emergent, and unpredictable. Our histories, inventions, ideas, and actions are also parts of the creative universe.'

So emergence does not just apply to biology. Political systems, economies and cities are examples of emergence – complex, self-organizing, unpredictably creative networks where everything is involved in a constant and complex interplay with everything else.

Science has only just begun to acknowledge such complexity of process but it is perfectly understandable by the Buddhist concept of *pratītya-samutpāda*, or interdependent co-arising, which claims that every occurrence has multiple causes and multiple effects, with the effects often acting as causes, and that things derive their nature from mutual dependence and are nothing in themselves. Many scientists now take a similar view, seeing reality as a vast force field in which every part influences every other part, with unpredictable consequences. For instance the physicist Henry Stapp in a 1971 report to the US Atomic Energy Commission: 'An elementary particle is not an independently existing unanalyzable entity. It is, in essence, a set of relationships that reach outward to other things.' Again, Bergson was far ahead, writing in 1907 of 'the universal interaction which, without doubt, is reality itself' and regarding even the inanimate world as a kind of giant organism:

So matter resolves itself into countless vibrations, all linked together in uninterrupted continuity, all influencing each other, and travelling in every direction like shivers through an immense body.

(*Matière et mémoire*, 1896)

All this has implications for everyday behaviour. If organisms are mutually dependent then it is wiser to cooperate than to dominate, and if life requires constant adaptation then nimble ingenuity is more effective than brute strength. If everything is connected to everything else then every action propagates its effects for ever, and if feedback loops are the method of propagation then every action also modifies the character of the actor. Many of these nano-modifications are below the level of perception but they eventually add up to a cumulative change that is all too perceptible. One day you may wake up and realize you have become a shithead – or, more likely, your partner wakes up and informs you of this, in a loud, outraged tone, en route to the door.

William James was good on this death by a thousand derelictions:

We are spinning our own fates, good or evil, and never to be undone. Every smallest stroke of virtue or of vice leaves its never so little scar. The drunken Rip Van Winkle, in Jefferson's play, excuses himself for every fresh dereliction by saying, 'I won't count this time!' Well! He may not count it; but it is being counted none the less. Down among his nerve-cells and fibres the molecules are counting it, registering and storing it up to be used against him when the next temptation comes. Nothing we ever do is, in strict scientific literalness, wiped out.

(*Psychology: The Briefer Course*, 1892)

But we can also spin our fates in a positive direction. We can choose to be Picasso rather than Rip Van Winkle. Bergson:

> Artisans of our lives, even artists when we so desire, we work continually, with the material provided by the past and present, by heredity and opportunity, to mould a figure, unique, new, original, and as unforeseeable as the form given by the sculptor to clay.
>
> (*La Pensée et le mouvant*, 1934)

The crucial word here is 'work'. No one can slump back on a sofa and expect to emerge. It is necessary to earn a living spiritually as well as materially. 'I value effort above everything,' Bergson said. And here is James, in *The Principles of Psychology*, written before becoming aware of Bergson:

> Our strength and our intelligence, our wealth and even our good luck, are things which warm our heart and make us feel ourselves a match for life. But deeper than all such things, and able to suffice unto itself without them, is the sense of the amount of effort which we can put forth ... He who can make none is but a shadow; he who can make much is a hero.
>
> (*The Principles of Psychology*, 1890)

For James, the truly heroic effort was not in rejection but in acceptance of circumstances often 'sinister and dreadful, unwelcome, incompatible with wished-for-things', in being able not merely to 'stand this universe' but 'still find a zest in it, not by ostrich-like forgetfulness, but by a pure inward willingness to take the world with those deterrent objects there'.

This effort is not only difficult but never-ending. To give life a specific goal is to render it lifeless. Bergson:

> It would be futile to try to assign to life a goal, in the human sense of the word. To speak of a goal is to think of a pre-existing model which need only be realized. It is to believe that all is given, that the future may be read in the present, and that life, in its entirety and movement, goes to work like our intellect, which takes merely a fragmentary and motionless view, and which naturally positions itself outside time.
>
> (*L'Évolution créatrice*, 1907)

William James described, with characteristic eloquence, the lack of satisfaction in attaining even the most desirable of goals:

> Everyone must at some time have wondered at that strange paradox of our moral nature, that, though the pursuit of outward good is the breath of

its nostrils, the attainment of outward good would seem to be its suffocation and death. Why does the painting of any paradise or Utopia, in heaven or on earth, awaken such yawnings? ... We look upon them from this delicious mess of insanities and realities, strivings and deadnesses, hopes and fears, agonies and exultations, which forms our present state, and *tedium vitae* is the only sentiment they awaken in our breasts ... Regarded as a stable finality, every outward good becomes a mere weariness to the flesh.

(*The Dilemma of Determinism*, 1884)

The lesson of the organism is that there is no respite from striving. And if constant striving is the meaning of life, then what we need most is energy. This is hardly surprising. As Bergson frequently reminded us, an organism has to work ceaselessly to find nutrients and convert them to energy:

Where does the energy come from? Ingested food, which is a kind of explosive, needing only the spark to discharge the energy it stores ... So all life, animal and vegetable, seems to be in essence an effort to accumulate energy and let it flow into flexible channels, changeable in nature, to accomplish infinitely varied kinds of work.

(*L'Évolution créatrice*, 1907)

Similarly, the life of an intelligent being requires mental energy. Buddha said, 'It is our own mind that should be made vigorous by energy', one of Bergson's books is called *Mind Energy* – and James delivered to the American Philosophical Association an inspirational and appropriately energetic lecture on the subject, *The Energies of Men*:

> I wish to spend this hour on one conception of functional psychology, a conception never once mentioned or heard of in laboratory circles, but used perhaps more than any other by common, practical men – I mean the conception of the *amount of energy available* for running one's mental and moral operations by. Practically everyone knows in his own person the difference between the days when the tide of this energy is high in him and those when it is low, though no one knows exactly what reality the term energy covers when used here, or what its tides, tensions and levels are in themselves . . . To have its level raised is the most important thing that can happen to a man, yet in all my reading I know of no single page or paragraph of a scientific psychology book in which it receives mention.
>
> (*The Energies of Men*, 1907)

This passage made me realize that one of the qualities I look for in literature is energy, that this quality is rare, and that, as James found with his psychologists, no literary critics or readers seem to value it – or even mention it. This must be because the twentieth century came to prize irony, obliquity and allusiveness and so regarded any form of passionate directness as naive. Any displays of gusto and exuberance would be especially embarrassing. So the richest energy sources I know are nineteenth-century writers such as Whitman and Browning, both unfashionable now but, in another exciting connection, both favourites of William James:

> Dramatic unities; laws of versification; ecclesiastical systems; scholastic doctrines. Bah! Give me Walt Whitman and Browning ten times over.
>
> (*The Letters of William James*, 1920)

Free, clean and renewable energy! Whitman and Browning are *fuel*!

'No end to learning,' Browning said in *A Grammarian's Funeral*, one of James's favourite poems. ('It always strengthens my backbone to read it.') Another lesson of the organism is that its necessary striving is always in order to learn. In the lower forms this learning is entirely utilitarian – and so is most human learning. Youth learns in order to have a career, middle age learns in order to advance this career, old age learns in order to avoid going gaga, and all stages like to display the fruits of learning as a mark of distinction. But the human organism has the sophistication to learn that if learning itself is the meaning of life, then it ought to learn to learn for the sake of the learning process itself. Another way to appreciate this is to remember that refusing to learn anything new is a major cause of petrifaction.

Expertise is another dangerously attractive end state. But both Bergson and James were lifelong novices, indefatigable learners, understanding that learning is endless and that, since everything is inseparably connected, learning must not be confined to any particular discipline (an example increasingly useful to counter the growing tyranny of the specialism). 'Life,' said William James, 'is one long eating of the fruit of the tree of knowledge.' Bergson's version:

> The philosopher is, first and foremost, someone who is always ready, at whatever age, to become a student once more.
>
> (*Mélanges*, 1972)

We are born to learn, as every child knows but most adults forget.

And the final lesson of the organism is that while life has no mission statement, no plan, no end state, and is entirely unpredictable, with no discernible unity ahead, it does have a unity behind. Every living thing has a history, which for lower organisms is embodied in the structure and for the human organism is character. This history influences but does not determine behaviour. Even simple organisms have choice, albeit limited, and the more sophisticated the organism, the wider the range of choice. For Bergson, the development of consciousness was essentially an expansion of choice. And while what is chosen is not determined, the choice determines character. 'We are what we do,' Bergson declared bluntly, prefiguring the existentialists.

Bergson himself did not develop this insight but James drew the obvious conclusion that it is possible to change character by changing behaviour. Only what we do matters and if we do things differently for long enough then eventually what has been artificial, willed and arduous will become genuine, instinctive and easy. It is not what we feel and think that guides what we do but what we do that guides what we feel and think, an insight known to psychology as self-conception theory and to self-help literature as, 'fake it till you make it'. James:

There is no more valuable precept in moral educa-tion than this, as all who have experience know: if we wish to conquer undesirable emotional tenden-cies in ourselves, we must assiduously, and in the first instance cold-bloodedly, go through the *outward motions* of those contrary dispositions we prefer to cultivate. The reward of persistency will infallibly come, in the fading out of the sullenness or depression, and the advent of real cheerfulness and kindliness in their stead. Smooth the brow, brighten the eye . . . and speak in a major key, pass the genial compliment, and your heart must be frigid indeed if it do not gradually thaw!

(What is an Emotion? 1884)

James exemplified this in his own life. His writing makes him sound like a born affirmer but the books came late in life (he was forty-eight when his first major work, *The Principles of Psychology,* was published). In his youth he suffered from severe depression and was even suicidal. The affirmation in his mature work was acquired, not innate, and it was only by prolonged thought and effort that he could finally experience a unique sense of joy at immersing in the oneness and flowing with the process.

When the healthy love of life is on one, and all its forms and its appetites seem so unutterably real; when the most brutal and the most spiritual things are lit by the same sun, and each is an integral part of the same richness – why, then it seems a grudging and sickly way of meeting so robust a universe to shrink away from any of its facts and wish them not to be. Rather take the strictly dramatic point of view, and treat the whole thing as a great unending romance which the spirit of the universe, striving to realize its own content, is eternally thinking out and representing to itself.

(The Dilemma of Determinism, 1884)

8

LEARNING TO EXPERIENCE MYSTICAL RAPTURES WITHOUT BECOMING ST TERESA

....

This emphasis on effort, creativity, energy and intensity is what distinguishes Bergson and James from most thinkers – and it is one of their greatest gifts. For there is a widespread tendency to see exalted states as irrational, dangerous and even delusional. However, as Bergson and James argued, what could be more rational than to seek the most satisfying levels of human experience?

But for the most part we believe the ultimate goods to be pleasure and well-being. It would be instructive to know what percentage of current media output is devoted to food, drink, sex, shopping and holidays. Not that I am arguing for asceticism. I enjoy as much as any a glass of wine and a good meal, and there are few experiences more consoling than tender, compassionate and companionable intercourse. I can also appreciate that all these pleasures may be even more agreeable in a warm and picturesque location by the sea. But such satisfactions are never enough.

Bergson argued that the pursuit of pleasure, comfort and luxury is one of the main problems of the modern world (a theme later taken up by Erich Fromm). William James described the experience of a week in a lakeside holiday resort 'equipped with means for satisfying all the necessary lower and most of the superfluous higher wants of man', in other words with a multitude of sporting, cultural and educational activities, good food and drink, and no disturbing poverty or crime. It sounds just like a luxury cruise:

> I went in curiosity for a day. I stayed for a week, held spellbound by the charm and ease of everything, by the middle-class paradise, without a sin, without a victim, without a blot, without a tear.
>
> And yet what was my own astonishment, on emerging into the dark and wicked world again, to catch myself quite unexpectedly and involuntarily saying 'Ouf! What a relief! Now for something primordial and savage, even though it were as bad as an Armenian massacre, to set the balance straight again. This order is too tame, this culture is too second-rate, this goodness too uninspiring. This human drama without a villain or a pang; this community so refined that ice-cream soda-water is the utmost offering it can make to the brute animal

in man; this city simmering in the tepid lakeside sun; this atrocious harmlessness of all things – I cannot abide with them. Let me take my chances again in the big outside worldly wilderness with all its sins and sufferings. There are the heights and depths, precipices and the steep ideals, the gleams of the awful and the infinite; and there is more hope and help a thousand times than in this dead level and quintessence of every mediocrity.

(*The Will to Believe*, 1897)

Well-being is also all very well – it must be the ground state – but it too is not enough. It has no 'gleams of the awful and the infinite', no heights. As Bergson put it:

Pleasure and well-being are something, joy is more ... The joy of enthusiasm involves much beyond the pleasure of well-being; the pleasure does not imply the joy, while the joy does imply and encompass the pleasure.

(*Les Deux Sources de la morale et de la religion*, 1932)

Yet contemporary aspiration rarely looks beyond the low-level satisfactions of pleasure and well-being. Joy offers an infinitely higher level of human experience but is one of those outdated words, like ardour, exaltation, sublimity and grace, that have become too embarrassingly naive for our sceptical, wised-up, agnostic age. Bergson explained how a word may diminish the experience it names – but discarding a word may suppress the corresponding experience. And why reject the supreme experience? Joy is even better than sex and does not require the cooperation of one or more consenting adults. Hark to this Bergson trumpet blast, which will surely awaken you from the slumber of contentment:

Philosophers who have speculated on the meaning of life and on the destiny of man have failed to take sufficient notice of an indication provided by nature itself. When our destiny is attained Nature alerts us by a clear sign. And that sign is joy. I mean joy, not pleasure. Pleasure is only a contrivance devised by nature to preserve life, and does not indicate the thrust and direction of life. But joy always announces that life has succeeded, gained ground, conquered. All great joy has a triumphant note. Now, if we follow this indication we find that wherever there is joy, there is creation; the richer the creation, the deeper the joy. The mother beholding her child is joyous, because she is conscious of having created it, physically and morally. The merchant developing his business, the manufacturer seeing his industry prosper, are joyous – is it because money is gained and reputation acquired? No doubt, riches and social position count for much, but it is pleasures rather than joy that they bring; the true joy is the feeling of having started an enterprise which flourishes, of having brought something to life. Take exceptional joys – the joy of the artist who has realized his thought, the joy of the thinker who has made a discovery or invention. It may be claimed that these work for glory and get the highest joy from the admiration they win. Profound error! We cling to praise and honours exactly because we are not sure of having succeeded. There is a touch of modesty in vanity. It is to reassure ourselves that we seek approbation; and just as we wrap the prematurely born child in cotton wool, so we gather round our work warm admiration to keep it alive. But he who is sure, absolutely sure, of having produced a work which will endure and live, cares no more for praise and feels above glory, because he is a creator and aware of it and so the joy he feels is the joy of a god. If in every field the triumph of life is creation, must we not suppose that human life has its goal in a creation which, unlike that of the artist and philosopher, may be pursued always by all – the creation of self by self, the developing of the personality by an effort which draws much from little, something from nothing, and adds unceasingly to whatever wealth the world contains?

(*L'Énergie spirituelle*, 1919)

The only adequate response to this is to leap up and cry *Hallelujah!* Emphasizing joy, and especially joy through self-creation, James and Bergson went to religion in search of the hallelujah factor. As Bergson said of his friend:

> The truth is that James leaned out upon the mystic, as, on a spring day, we lean out to feel on our cheeks the caress of the breeze, or as, by the sea, we watch sailing boats to know how the wind blows. Souls filled with religious enthusiasm are truly lifted up and carried away: why could they not enable us too to experience directly, as in a scientific experiment, this uplifting and exalting force?
>
> (*La Pensée et le mouvant*, 1934)

The problem is that religion tends to divide people into hostile camps – the passionate believers and the equally passionate rejecters. For most of my life I have belonged in the second camp but first James and then Bergson showed that this was throwing out the re-born infant along with the holy water. It may be possible to enjoy the benefits of religion without subscribing to an orthodox faith.

Bergson went straight to the heart of the problem by distinguishing between the good and bad in religion. The origin of morality, he argued, is the social code imposed by the group.

> The social instinct ... at the basis of social obligation always has in view ... a closed society, however large.
>
> *(Les Deux Sources de la morale et de la religion*, 1932)

The group may be a clan or a tribe or a nation but it is always closed and always acts in its own interest and against the interests of other groups.

> Who can help seeing that social cohesion is largely due to a community's need to protect itself against others, and that it is primarily as against all others that we love those with whom we live?
>
> *(Les Deux Sources de la morale et de la religion*, 1932)

In fact the group always sees itself as superior to other groups:

> The individual does not obey merely from habit or fear of punishment; the group must, of course, exalt itself above the others, if only to rouse courage in battle, and the consciousness of this superiority of strength secures greater strength, as well as all the satisfactions of pride ... Think of all the pride and moral energy that made up the *civis Romanus sum*: self-respect in the Roman citizen must have been

what we call nationalism today. But we need not turn
to history to see self-respect coinciding with group
pride. We need only observe what goes on under our
eyes in the smaller societies which form within the
bigger one, drawing people together by the distinguishing badge of a real or apparent superiority
separating them from the common herd.

(*Les Deux Sources de la morale
et de la religion*, 1932)

So the group religion reinforces cohesion by assuring
the group members of their superiority. This is why
religion and nationalism are such perfect allies – they
are both expressions of group narcissism. And when
the superiority of the group, a given that demands
universal acceptance, is challenged and even rejected,
possibly even *mocked*, the group naturally becomes
enraged and goes on the offensive.

This view of the group is a useful lesson for our
own age, which tends to value group allegiance as an
unqualified good, a provider of identity and community, and fails to see the separatism and belligerence.
There are so many inviting groups now, based on work,
peers, gender, race, political and sexual orientation,
special interest, as well as a welter of new religions to
add to the old.

Bergson had no illusions about the excesses of
closed religion:

> The spectacle of what religions have been in the
> past, and of what some religions still are to this day,
> is indeed humiliating for human intelligence. What
> a mess of error and folly! Experience may say, 'that
> is false', and reasoning, 'this is preposterous', but
> humanity only clings all the more to that absurdity
> and error. And if only this were all! But religion has
> been known to encourage immorality and even to
> prescribe crime.
>
> (*Les Deux Sources de la morale
> et de la religion*, 1932)

A few years after writing this Bergson had personal
experience of the crimes committed in the name of
group superiority – when the Nazis invaded France
and he felt obliged to refuse exemption from the anti-
Jewish laws. It must have been a bitter irony that, after
denouncing the group mentality, the only way to reject
a conquering group was to renew the renounced affilia-
tion to his own group. So often circumstances conspire
to drive the free back into the tribe.

It is difficult to reject group superiority because this
is not only innate but immensely reassuring, possibly
the most effective comfort blanket for adults, and so
relinquishing such immense comfort requires an even
more immense and continuing effort. Group superiority will always develop rationalizations in its defence
but is entirely emotional in its origin and effect. This is

why there is nothing more futile than trying to reason with the self-righteous – and why there is no one more dangerous than the self-righteous, who are not only convinced that their beliefs are eternal truth but would also impose them on others by force if given the opportunity. James:

> The first thing to learn in intercourse with others is non-interference with their own peculiar ways of being happy, provided those ways do not assume to interfere by violence with ours. No one has insight into all the ideals. No one should presume to judge them offhand. The pretension to dogmatize about them is the root of most human injustices and cruelties, and the trait in human character most likely to make the angels weep.
>
> (*The Will to Believe*, 1897)

But if tolerance is so difficult to understand and practise, how was the concept ever born? The answer lies in the open, dynamic religion of the individual, which every now and then breaks free from the closed, static religion of the group. Bergson described such individuals as:

> moral creators who see in their mind's eye a new social atmosphere, an environment in which life would be more worth living, so that if people tried

it they would refuse to go back to the old customs. This is the only way to define moral progress, but it is only in retrospect that it can be so defined, when some exceptional moral nature has created a new feeling, like a new kind of music, and passed it on to mankind, stamped with his own vitality.

(*Les Deux Sources de la morale et de la religion*, 1932)

Only Bergson could see moral example as 'a new kind of music'. But the key word is 'example'. These moral 'creators' convert not by preaching but by *vitality*. A mindset based on emotion may be changed only by a more powerful emotion. Preaching is futile:

We cannot repeat too often that it is not by preaching love of our neighbour that we can achieve it . . . The truth is that heroism may be the only way to love. And heroism cannot be preached, it can only reveal itself, when its mere presence may stir others to action. For heroism itself is a return to movement, and comes from an emotion – infectious like all emotions – similar to the creative act.

(*Les Deux Sources de la morale et de la religion*, 1932)

It is probably true that only heroes or heroines have the courage to challenge the group openly – but, inspired by the example of the heroic, the unheroic may secretly and silently defect.

For Bergson the two greatest moral creators were Socrates and Christ – and it is significant that neither left any writings (Socrates believed that writing things down was a disastrous innovation). They inspired by force of vitality alone. When I read the New Testament as an adult, after many years of avoidance because of the insensitive way it was taught, it was the vitality of Christ that surprised me, so different from the iconography with the outstretched entreating hands and sorrowful, submissive expression. The other surprise was the inconsistency, the many contradictions, which Christians never acknowledge, much less explain – for instance, as well as the famous admonition to turn the other cheek there is the less familiar battle cry: 'I came not to send peace, but a sword.' Bergson argued that the contradictions, paradoxes and absurdly impractical exhortations are not a problem but *part of the appeal*:

The morality of the Gospels is essentially that of the open soul: are we not justified in pointing out that, in its clearest admonitions, it borders on paradox, and even on contradiction? If riches are an evil, would we not corrupt the poor by giving them all we possess? If the injured turn the other cheek, what becomes of justice? But the paradox and contradiction disappear if we consider that the purpose of these maxims is to create a certain disposition of the soul. It is not for the poor but for his own sake that the rich man should give away his riches: blessed are the poor in spirit! The beauty is not in depriving oneself but in not feeling deprived. The act by which the soul opens out broadens and raises to spirituality a morality enclosed in precise rules.

(*Les Deux Sources de la morale et de la religion*, 1932)

This is open religion, more like artistic improvising than the laying down of doctrine. James too rejected the idea of eternal moral truth:

There is no such thing possible as an ethical philosophy dogmatically made up in advance ... There can be no final truth in ethics any more than in physics.

(*The Will to Believe*, 1897)

As Bergson pointed out, belief in universal human rights, the mantra of the Western world and assumed to be the inevitable terminus of its history, was not an eternal truth awaiting discovery but a human *invention* – and a *religious* invention. Philosophy had never proposed such a thing and, without Christianity, might never have done so. And democracy, assumed to be the inevitable outcome of the inevitable belief, is not in the least natural but an idea that had to be created and imposed.

Bergson also understood that religion is not an all-or-nothing commitment:

> Along with the souls who follow the mystic path to the end there are many who go at least part of the way . . . William James used to say that he had never experienced mystical states but that if he ever heard them mentioned 'something within answered the call'. Most of us are probably in the same boat.
>
> (*Les Deux Sources de la morale et de la religion*, 1932)

Many of us would like to have the raptures and visions without the need to become Joan of Arc. I certainly have no urge to convert the pagan hordes watching *MasterChef* and *A Place in the Sun* – but I need something more satisfying than stuffing myself and lying on a beach.

James took the typically pragmatic view that the mystical state should not be surrendered to the religious but may be available to even the most rational and secular. For a spiritual experience is merely perception heightened to maximum intensity, turbo perception, an engagement so different from everyday experience that it seems like the intervention of an other-worldly force. But there is no such force and the experience does not require special circumstances. Any setting will do:

Mystical states merely add a supersensuous meaning to the ordinary outward data of consciousness. They are excitements like the emotions of love or ambition, gifts to our spirit by means of which facts already objectively before us fall into a new expressiveness and make a new connection with our active life. They do not contradict these facts as such, or deny anything that our senses have immediately seized. It is the rationalistic critic rather who plays the part of denier in the controversy, and his denials have no strength, for there never can be a state of facts to which new meaning may not truthfully be added, provided the mind ascend to a more enveloping point of view.

(*The Varieties of Religious Experience*, 1902)

And this 'supersensuous meaning' is a profoundly satisfying sense of oneness:

The keynote of it is invariably a reconciliation. It is as if the opposites of the world, whose contradictoriness and conflict make all our difficulties and troubles, were melted into unity . . . the *other* in its various forms appears absorbed into the One.

(*The Varieties of Religious Experience*, 1902)

The states vary in duration and intensity but the feeling, though impossible to justify or even define, always combines comfort and awe, the reassurance of returning home and a wonder at the immensity and grandeur of home:

> Mystical states indeed wield no authority due simply to their being mystical states. But the higher ones among them point in directions to which the religious sentiments even of non-mystical men incline. They tell of the supremacy of the ideal, of vastness, of union, of safety, and of rest. They offer us *hypotheses*, hypotheses which we may voluntarily ignore, but which as thinkers we cannot possibly upset. The supernaturalism and optimism to which they would persuade us may, interpreted in one way or another, be after all the truest insights into the meaning of this life.
>
> (*The Varieties of Religious Experience*, 1902)

The higher levels are difficult to attain but there is an entry level available to everyone. Unlike most writers on spiritual experience, James acknowledged that alcoholic intoxication is a mystical state, albeit a rather coarse one. Try partnering this passage with a glass of Sancerre:

> Sobriety diminishes, discriminates, and says no; drunkenness expands, unites, and says yes. It is in fact the great inciter of the *Yes* function in man. It brings its votary from the chill periphery of things to

the radical core. It makes him for the moment one with truth. Not through mere perversity do men run after it. To the poor and unlettered it stands in the place of symphony concerts and of literature; and it is part of the deeper mystery and tragedy of life that whiffs and gleams of something that we immediately recognize as excellent should be vouchsafed to so many of us only in the fleeting earlier phases of what in its totality is so degrading a poisoning. The drunken consciousness is one bit of the mystic consciousness, and our total opinion of it must find its place in our opinion of that larger whole.

(*The Varieties of Religious Experience*, 1902)

A glass or two of alcohol may bring whiffs and gleams but for the full 3D and HD experience James advocated spiritual exercises such as those of Ignatius Loyola, founder of the Jesuits, or Buddhism. However, even a change of attitude may be enough to intensify experience. As well as religious belief there is vision, a personal way of perceiving the world. Like Bergson, James believed that this is essential ('where there is no vision the people perish') and that philosophy should be the provider: 'philosophy is more a matter of passionate vision than of logic'. The problem is that 'few professorial philosophers have any vision'. Both Bergson and James were professors but neither was remotely professorial.

Bergson's vision was pantheistic. He talked of Nature wanting this and doing that and constantly creating, but made it clear that such language was figurative – he did not believe in a Nature with intentions and plans:

> Nature is more and better than a plan in the course of implementation. A plan is a term given to a project: it closes the future whose form it defines. But the portals of the future stay wide open before the evolution of life. It is a creation that continues forever as a consequence of its original impetus. This movement is the unity of the connected world – a prolific unity, infinitely rich, and superior to any the intellect could imagine, because the intellect is merely one of its products.
>
> (*L'Évolution créatrice*, 1907)

Nor did Bergson attempt to construct a pantheistic system, though he compared the movement of life to a consciousness.

> Now, the more we fix our attention on this continuity of life, the more we see that organic evolution resembles the evolution of a consciousness, in which the past pushing into the present causes a new form of awareness, incommensurable with what went before.
>
> (*L'Évolution créatrice*, 1907)

The belief that the world is suffused with consciousness is panpsychism – and this attracted William James, though again more as a vision, a hypothesis, than a fully elaborated belief. Like pantheism, it provides a richer and more vital sense of belonging in the world, a way of experiencing not just pleasure but joy. It seems that, for our necessary spiritual nourishment, it helps to have some sort of pan to fry the day's catch in.

CONCLUSION:
BERGSON'S CASH VALUE

....

All Bergson's work was inspired by a conviction that life is petrified and diminished by theories, categories and conventions, and that it is the purpose of philosophy not to add yet more abstract reasoning but to restore awareness of lived life – to renew, revitalize and enrich direct contact with the world. Theory is useful only as a way back to experience.

So he practised philosophy to escape philosophy, thought rationally in order to question rationalism and wrote in order to subvert language. Always he strove to recover the experiencing self that is constantly being suppressed, often to the point of extinction, by a trio of powerful bullies – the categorizing, utilitarian and social selves. And always he sought to protect the evolving self from finality, rigidity and circumscription, privileging the dynamic over the static, the holistic over the compartmentalized, the organic over the mechanical, the qualitative over the quantitative, the intuitive over the analytic, the continuing over the completed, the open over the closed and, above all, the free over the determined. And what greater gift could a philosopher offer than to restore us to ourselves and the world, and then to send us forth once more, re-energized and renewed, with a vital sense of freedom and even of creativity and joy?

> Philosophy gains by finding some absolute in the moving world of phenomena. But we too shall gain in our feeling of greater joy and strength. Greater joy because the reality invented before our eyes will give each of us, unceasingly, some of the satisfactions which art gives at rare intervals to the privileged; it will reveal to us, beyond the fixity and monotony which our senses, hypnotized by constant need, at first perceived in it, ever-recurring novelty, the moving originality of things. But above all we shall have greater strength, for we shall feel that we are participating, creators of ourselves, in the great work of creation . . . By getting hold of itself, our ability to act will become intensified. Until now humbled in an attitude of obedience, slaves of vaguely-felt natural necessities, we shall stand once more erect.
>
> (*La Pensée et le mouvant*, 1934)

Appreciating the universal work of creation demands the use of every means available. So Bergson reunited the three ways of seeking understanding of life, increasingly separate and often mutually hostile –

religion, science and the humanities – or, rather, he behaved as though these had never gone their separate ways. Within science he embraced physics, chemistry and biology. Within the humanities he embraced psychology, sociology and politics and, within the arts, literature, painting and music. Within philosophy itself he embraced many ideas that have since developed into separate specialisms. He was a processist celebrating fluidity, a pantheist celebrating oneness, an emergentist celebrating creativity, a phenomenologist celebrating pure being and an existentialist celebrating personal freedom and choice. Buy one philosopher and get at least four free.

And, unknown to himself, he provides another kind of historical unity by linking the very old ideas of oriental religion with the very new theories of Western science. Separated by thousands of years and miles, and immersed in utterly different branches of utterly different cultures, the scientist in the white coat turns out to be the monk in orange robes.

Bergson's ideas, once so radical and controversial, are now everywhere – and how ironic that the man who rejected the very possibility of prediction should have accidently made so many accurate predictions.

Bergson also rejected eternal truth but, while his concepts of unity and process may not be eternal, their power to encourage and console has remained undiminished over millennia. There is no more thrilling inspiration than the creativity of process ('Life transcends finality') and no greater comfort than enfoldment in unity ('The philosopher neither obeys nor commands but seeks only to be at one with nature').

These two concepts of unity and process offer the apparently contradictory desiderata of security and adventure, showing us how to be at home in the world while remaining independent and free. They restore to us both immanence and imminence and teach us not just to be, but to belong and become.

HOMEWORK

INTRODUCTION
....

There was no biography of Bergson until 1997 (*Bergson* by Philippe Soulez and Frédérique Worms, Flammarion) and this account is disappointingly short and dull – the momentous meeting with William James does not even get a mention. On the other hand *William James: In the Maelstrom of American Modernism* by Robert D. Richardson (Houghton Mifflin, 2007) is a marvellous biography, packed with telling detail and great quotes and written with insight, style, wit and enthusiasm. The same author has also edited a lively selection of James's most readable pieces, *The Heart of William James* (Harvard University Press, 2010). The equivalent Bergson anthology is *Henri Bergson: Key Writings*, edited by Keith Ansell Pearson and John Mullarkey (Continuum, 2002), which includes substantial extracts from Bergson's major books, along with some of his finest essays (for instance *The Perception of Change* and *The Possible and the Real*) and also his correspondence with William James. The introduction to this volume provides a lucid and cogent summary of Bergson's thought.

1

LEARNING TO SWING ALONG WITH THE PROCESS

....

Bergson used the word 'process' all through his work but made the fatal mistake of never putting it in a book title, so Alfred North Whitehead's *Process and Reality* (1929) is usually regarded as the foundation of modern process philosophy. But Whitehead's book is generally acknowledged as hard going. For a simple explanation of a simple idea try *Process Metaphysics: an Introduction to Process Philosophy* by Nicholas Rescher (State University of New York, 1996). There are also many interesting process websites, for instance that of the Center for Process Studies (www.ctr4process.org), which offers free of charge many of the articles from its journal, *Process Studies*.

As for swinging along with an actual process, the apparently simple act of walking is in fact a complex experience of unity in process, combining seeing, hearing, rumination and flow. Both Bergson and James were prodigious walkers.

2

LEARNING TO TUNE IN TO
THE MELODY OF DURATION

....

It is a striking vindication of the relevance of Bergson's ideas that so many of them are being explored in

contemporary books, though usually without acknow-
ledging Bergson. The Claudia Hammond survey is
described in *Time Warped: Unlocking the Mysteries of
Time Perception* (Canongate, 2012), which draws on
contemporary research into the subjective experience
of time (Bergson's duration). Adam Frank's *About Time*
(Oneworld, 2011) is a cultural history, showing how the
perception of time has changed radically through the
ages, culminating in the tyranny of clock time.

3
LEARNING TO HEED THE WHISPERS OF INTUITION
....

The power of intuition has also been recognized
recently in books such as *Blink: the Power of Thinking
without Thinking* by Malcolm Gladwell (Penguin,
2006), *Gut Feelings: the Intelligence of the Unconscious*
by Gerd Gigerenzer (Penguin, 2008) and *The Decisive
Moment* by Jonah Lehrer (Canongate, 2010). These
books are concerned mainly with instantaneous
decision-making, often in areas of specialized expertise.

A universally relevant use of intuition is in learning
to evaluate people swiftly by seeing through pleasant-
ries and charm. A good training exercise is a game
known as Spot the Nasty, which I learned many years
ago from a lively woman at a wedding reception. The
idea is to apply intuition to well-known people in order
to identify those who are really the opposite of their

public personas. The players make separate lists and then compare notes. When the woman and I did this at the wedding both lists had the same name at the top: Jimmy Savile. The game is better with dead celebrities, where there is often corroborative evidence to be found in biographies. As a boy I always found the sugary sentimentality of Walt Disney deeply fraudulent and so I was thrilled to discover as an adult that Disney was indeed thoroughly nasty.

4
LEARNING TO LAUGH THROUGH
DEPARTMENT MEETINGS

....

The easiest way into Bergson's oeuvre (never obscure but often densely argued in a way that requires concentrated effort) is his little book *Laughter: an Essay on the Meaning of the Comic* (Doubleday, 1956). Yet this book is usually dismissed by Bergson's commentators for being 'popular'. *Key Writings* is a bulky anthology of 400 pages but contains nothing from *Laughter*. Gilles Deleuze's highly regarded *Bergsonism* (Zone Books, 1988) does not even include *Laughter* in its list of Bergson's works (which is one reason why I do not share in the high regard). These are examples of philosophy's usual disdain for the comic vision. (Wittgenstein once considered writing a philosophy book consisting entirely of jokes, an intriguing project that, alas, never got as far as the first joke.) Few philosophers are funny and Bergson himself is no exception (the jokes quoted in *Laughter* are woefully bad) but his advice to interpret life as high comedy seems to me both sophisticated and practical. For instance, one way to alleviate the agony of work meetings is to treat them as satirical one-act plays staged expressly for your entertainment.

5

LEARNING TO KNOW WHAT WE KNOW BUT DO NOT SEE THAT WE KNOW AND TO SEE WHAT WE SEE BUT DO NOT KNOW THAT WE SEE

....

The homework for this section could fill a book in itself and take a lifetime to complete. So many great books, plays, paintings, photographs and films! But what discourages contemptuous labelling more than anything else is an artwork that encourages empathy with a despicable character. Few works succeed in this difficult feat but one is Bruce Robinson's film *Withnail and I*, whose main character is an irresponsible alcoholic, braggart, coward, liar and thief – yet impossible to despise. The film's humour is based on convincing detail and so it also illustrates Bergson's theory of comedy and can serve as additional homework for the previous section. Complete one assignment but give yourself two grades.

6

LEARNING TO ENHANCE PERCEPTION, MEMORY AND ATTENTION

....

If a crucial skill is the ability to make unfamiliar associations and this is a function of the brain's right hemisphere, which is responsible for imagination, humour and spirituality, then anything that encourages any of these three is useful. So the William James dot exercise in this chapter could be improved by finding more right-hemisphere associations, seeing the dot as the last full stop in Joyce's *Ulysses*, or as God's view of planet earth, or one's own significance in the eyes of senior management.

7

LEARNING TO BE, AND BELONG TO, AN ORGANISM

....

Reinventing the Sacred by Stuart A. Kauffman (Basic Books, 2008) provides a good summary of the scientific evidence, largely but not solely biological, for the new paradigm of emergence which interprets life as ceaseless creativity. After establishing that life is emergent, Kauffman goes on to apply the paradigm to national economies and human consciousness. The physicist Fritjof Capra performs a similar exercise in *The Web of Life* (Flamingo, 1996) but stresses the cooperative nature of emergence, its dependence on the connections of everything to everything else. So the evolutionary theory that life is a competition won by the powerful and ruthless has had to be modified to allow for the fact that the powerful and ruthless usually destroy their habitats and perish – and evolution has become co-evolution, which recognizes that it is much more effective to cut a deal and work out a mutually beneficial arrangement. Similarly, the deterministic genetics that viewed the organism simply as a carrier for genes, and the habitat as simply a stage for the acting out of the script encoded in the genes, has had to become epigenetics, which understands that it is all much more complicated, and that, via multiple feedback loops, habitat influences genes and genes influence each other and their habitat (see *The Epigenetics Revolution* by Nessa Carey, Icon Books, 2012).

For an injection of poetic rocket fuel and a jubilant celebration of unity in process, try Whitman's 'Crossing Brooklyn Ferry', another favourite of William James.

8
LEARNING TO EXPERIENCE MYSTICAL RAPTURES
WITHOUT BECOMING ST TERESA
....

Pantheism seems to be the hypothesis most conducive to joy, because thinkers and writers with this orientation (for instance Spinoza and Wordsworth) are usually affirmative. For pantheistic mysticism at its most ecstatic try the thirteenth-century Sufi poet Jelaluddin Rumi (*The Essential Rumi* translated by Coleman Barks, Penguin, 1999). Rumi was also the creator of the whirling dervish dance and partial to wine so, if good translations had been available, Bergson and James would surely have loved him (little is known of Bergson's private life, but a visitor to the Bergson home was surprised by the great thinker's fondness for champagne). The homework exercise is to experience mystical unity in process by reading a few lines of Rumi, drinking a glass of champagne and doing a whirling dervish dance.

ACKNOWLEDGEMENTS

....

I would like to thank Jennifer Christie for many invaluable suggestions.